Cambridge Elements

Elements in Sociolinguistics
edited by
Rajend Mesthrie
University of Cape Town
Valerie Fridland
University of Nevada, Reno

CONVERSATIONS WITH STRANGERS

William Labov
University of Pennsylvania
with
Gillian Sankoff
University of Pennsylvania

CAMBRIDGE
UNIVERSITY PRESS

CAMBRIDGE
UNIVERSITY PRESS

Shaftesbury Road, Cambridge CB2 8EA, United Kingdom

One Liberty Plaza, 20th Floor, New York, NY 10006, USA

477 Williamstown Road, Port Melbourne, VIC 3207, Australia

314–321, 3rd Floor, Plot 3, Splendor Forum, Jasola District Centre,
New Delhi – 110025, India

103 Penang Road, #05–06/07, Visioncrest Commercial, Singapore 238467

Cambridge University Press is part of Cambridge University Press & Assessment,
a department of the University of Cambridge.

We share the University's mission to contribute to society through the pursuit of
education, learning and research at the highest international levels of excellence.

www.cambridge.org
Information on this title: www.cambridge.org/9781009340939

DOI: 10.1017/9781009340922

© William Labov and Gillian Sankoff 2023

First published 2023

A catalogue record for this publication is available from the British Library.

ISBN 978-1-009-34093-9 Paperback
ISSN 2754-5539 (online)
ISSN 2754-5520 (print)

Additional resources for this publication at
www.cambridge.org/conversationswithstrangers.

Conversations with Strangers

Elements in Sociolinguistics

DOI: 10.1017/9781009340922
First published online: July 2023

William Labov
University of Pennsylvania
with
Gillian Sankoff
University of Pennsylvania

Author for correspondence: William Labov, labov@comcast.net

Abstract: This Element documents the evolution of a research program that began in the early 1960s with the author's first investigation of language change on Martha's Vineyard. It traces the development of what has become the basic framework for studying language variation and change. Interviews with strangers are the backbone of this research: the ten American English speakers appearing here were all strangers to the interviewer at the time. They were selected as among the most memorable, from thousands of interviews across six decades. The speakers express their ideas and concerns in the language of everyday life, dealing with their way of earning a living, getting along with neighbors, raising a family – all matters in which their language serves them well. These people speak for themselves. And you will hear their voices. What they have to say is a monument to the richness and variety of the American vernacular, offering a tour of the studies that have built the field of sociolinguistics.

Keywords: sociolinguistics, Labov, dialect, speech style, recording

ISBNs: 9781009340939 (PB), 9781009340922 (OC)
ISSNs: 2754-5539 (online), 2754-5520 (print)

Contents

> They can be complete strangers
> and they ask you if you want a lift.
>
> Rose Barrise, September 1963

1 Prologue: What This Element Is About

Conversations with Strangers presents interviews with ten speakers of the English language who were strangers to the interviewer at the time. Its sections deal with the speakers' ways of earning a living, getting along with their neighbors, raising a family: all matters in which their language served them well.

Few sociolinguists have introduced us to the speakers they have recorded by citing extensive excerpts from their speech in their published materials. One notable exception is Macaulay (1991, 2005), who has highlighted the eloquence of the people he recorded in Ayrshire. *Conversations with Strangers* goes one step farther, in allowing readers also to be hearers of the speakers. For each of the ten people, the text reproduces excerpts from the interviews in printed form, and their voices can also be heard, as often as you hit the "Play" button. These ten speakers are not the products of higher education, and their life experience differs in many ways from that of the interviewer. The success of the interview is registered by their willingness to share that experience.

This Element was written at a time when the COVID-19 pandemic had effectively ruled out such face-to-face exchanges with strangers. It shows how much can be gained if the situation should return to normal and the stranger once again becomes the target of our research. The Sociolinguistics Archive at the University of Pennsylvania Library holds some 7,500 recordings made over the past sixty years, including over 1,000 interviews where I was the interviewer.

Those who rarely speak with strangers may not have had the opportunity to hear the full force of the English language enlisted to promote the doctrines that they favor, or decry those they think most pernicious. *Conversations with Strangers* is addressed not only to people who want to do sociolinguistic research, but to people who would like to talk to strangers, but don't quite know how; to students of the American language, students in English classes, and students of eloquence. People who talk to a good many strangers may find common themes in their experience and that of ourselves and our students.

Recordings of native speakers of American English are at the heart of this publication. What I have to say about them is in my own English, which has nothing hard to understand in it. I have avoided the special technical vocabulary of my parent discipline, linguistics – even when I am writing about the varieties of English that Americans use when they are approached from out of the blue by somebody who talks like me. These ten are not pretending to be a representative sample of Americans or any group or type of American speakers. I have chosen them because I thought they had a great deal to say and had their own way of saying it.

True enough, this research began with studies of regional dialects. But you will find that these early interviews were very much concerned with what the speakers had learned from a lifetime of experience. Only a few minutes of every interview were devoted to differences in words or sounds.[1]

Every field of study needs an introduction to its basic elements, to the rules that put those elements together, and to the research strategies that scientists use to make progress in the field. For me, the pursuit of linguistics promised a way to better understand the nature of human language. However, the research methods used in mid-twentieth century linguistics did not involve the observation of language in its natural habitat: as used all day, every day in daily life.

My aim was to observe how people talked when they were not being observed. This involved a problem, well known in other fields as the "observer effect." I referred to it as the "observer's paradox" since it can never be solved completely. In some of the examples to follow, we will see how my own efforts at reducing the differences in style between working people and researchers developed over the years. In a 1984 paper, I summarized some of these recommendations to fieldworkers:

> One of the crucial elements that determine the course of a sociolinguistic interview ... is the relative degree of authority of the interviewer and speaker ... The interviewer is engaged in an occupation that clearly points to membership in a middle class institution of some kind – research or journalism. Sociolinguistic interviewers must continually monitor their behavior for any signs of this authority. They must review their lexical and grammatical choices to remove any signs of bookishness or of literary language ... The interviewer must have a keen appreciation of the strengths and expertise of the speaker, a genuine and profound interest in what the speaker knows. (Labov 1984: 40)

In my first research project on the island of Martha's Vineyard, I developed two innovative strategies in using the language of everyday speech as the raw material for linguistic analysis. The first involved the use of the tape recorder. In the early decades of the twentieth century, various methods of recording speech had been used by dialectologists, and the recordings had become a standard part of the records they kept. And by the early 1950s, American linguists had begun to use

---

[1] Readers who would like further information on these and other differences may want to consult the *Atlas of North American English* (Labov, Ash, and Boberg 2006) to see where these sounds are to be heard in different parts of the country.

the tape recorder to record the Indigenous languages of North America (Voegelin and Harris 1951). Recording conversations, rather than elicited words or phrases, yielded data on speech in its natural context of language use, and my plan was to use this data to analyze the sound system. At that time, the analysis of vowel sounds was done with the Kay Sonograph.[2] I was a student in a course taught at Columbia by Franklin Cooper of Haskins Laboratories in 1962. I asked him whether the Kay Sonograph could be adopted for the study of dialect differences in the field. He said no, the noise level in the field was too high.

Undaunted, I turned to the high-quality Nagra recorder recommended by my film maker friend Murray Lerner, and I found that my Martha's Vineyard recordings did allow me to study the entire range of speech sounds in the spoken language. The crucial concept I came up with was the *linguistic variable*, a construct that provided for "different ways of pronouncing the same thing," and was subject to quantitative analysis.

In the Martha's Vineyard project, I had started out using the methods traditionally employed in research on dialects of English (particularly out-of-the-way dialects): interviewing knowledgeable speakers,[3] collecting words and phrases unique to that dialect (often traditional words that were going out of fashion), and describing the dialect in its particularities. Here again, Murray's example steered me in a different direction. This second innovation benefited from his advice on how to generate the conversations to be recorded. With his camera on his shoulder, Murray put questions to people that led them to speak about the most important issues in their lives.[4] Now listening again to the people I recorded more than sixty years ago, I am transported into the living past as it moves ahead.

In good dialectological tradition, I called on the editor of the local newspaper for recommendations on who I might talk to. He recommended the fisherman

---

[2] The Kay Sonograph has since been replaced by several generations of computer-based analyses of vowel formant measurements, first by the hardware-implemented Linear Predictive Coding analysis in the 1980s. Software advances since that time have facilitated the routines for vowel measurement (e.g. PRAAT, ESPS [Entropic Signal Processing System]). However, selecting the words containing a given vowel and choosing the point in time for formant measurement remained time-consuming until the development of programs for forced alignment and automatic formant measurements. Measurement has also been enhanced by the FAVE (Forced Alignment and Vowel Extraction) program suite (Rosenfelder et al. 2012).

[3] An example of this research strategy is cited by Macaulay in describing the methods of dialectologists in the early twentieth century, noting that an earlier scholar had based his account of Ayrshire pronunciation entirely on five elderly "authorities" who lived in Tarbolton. (Macaulay 1991: 30)

[4] Many of Murray Lerner's documentary films focused on music: In *Festival* (1967), he initiated conversations with musicians and audience members at the Newport Folk Festival, encouraging the youthful counter-cultural audience members emerging from sleeping bags on the beach to express what the music meant to them as a rejection of the values of the previous generation.

Donald Poole (the focus of Section 3), whom I interviewed then and on several following occasions. From there I branched out to others recommended by Poole, a method sometimes referred to as the "snowball" or 'friend of a friend" technique (Milroy 1987: 66; Tagliamonte 2006; Schilling 2013). But along the way, I discovered that I didn't need introductions: I could introduce myself to people in other towns all over the island as a stranger, and have successful conversations with them.

1.1 First Steps

A first step in any sociolinguistic investigation is to locate local speakers who are "not doing anything," likely to be found on stoops, benches, porches, docks, and parks. The linguist then makes eye contact with that person and says, more or less: "I wonder if you could help me out a few minutes?" The answer is rarely negative: most people do respond positively. It generates an acknowledgment that entitles the linguist to enter into a state of talk with someone who is no longer a stranger.

It must be admitted that there is a price to be paid: in approaching strangers you might well be refused. Say that the refusal rate – people who say no, I'm not interested – may be as high as one third. This isn't so bad, as projects go, but it should be admitted that no matter how many warm and friendly receptions you receive, the next refusal will hurt. Those who are too busy, or don't know you from Adam may be substantial setbacks in your love affair with the human race. But long experience shows that the strangers who open their doors will make up for those who close them. These ten sections are submitted in support of this thesis.

1.2 What to Talk About

We encourage speakers to talk about the most serious events of their lives. This might involve the danger of death, or the other events that made them the people they are. One penetrating question has been "If there was one thing that happened to you in your life that you would never forget, what would that be?" Bill Peters' (Section 6) answer to that question was a memorable response that brought out his personal philosophy of independence.

One general principle is that conflict is more interesting than harmony. Many fieldworkers have made a profitable beginning with the question "Is this a friendly neighborhood?" It may turn out that the negative trumps the positive. Though you are a stranger to the neighborhood, it will do you no harm to learn about it, and your conversational partners may find that they had a lot to say that never came out before.

1.3 How to Listen

The fieldworker listens to what the other has to say. The success of the enterprise depends upon both parties overlooking the likelihood that the person operating the tape recorder may have a different view of the causes of community conflict, race, religion, the imminence of the supernatural, and gender equality. The remarkable feature of these conversations is that community members are so willing to overlook and forgive these differences between the investigators and themselves.

The advent of the coronavirus pandemic has brought this program to a stop. Strangers can still be seen sitting on city stoops, park benches, washing their cars, leaning out of windows. But no field workers are to be seen approaching them. The coronavirus severed us from that world of free communication that made every stranger a potential neighbor, and we have moved into an historical period that has strongly reinforced the longstanding prohibition of our parents: don't talk to strangers. *Conversations with Strangers* will show what can be gained when fieldwork in the speech community will return to common practice. We don't know how long it will be before we can resume the free approach to strangers that is the trademark of our research.

1.4 Why These?

This Element features ten conversations with strangers, eight where the interviewer was me and two where the interviewers were my students. Nine of the people lived in the eastern part of the country. Only one, Brad Anders (Section 7), who ran a farm near Salt Lake City, Utah, was located in the western United States.

The ten speakers were selected from a much larger number in the Sociolinguistic Archive. They were recognized early on as extraordinary, because of what they had to say and how they said it. Twenty years ago, three of these ten were selected for inclusion in the "Classic Sociolinguistic Interviews" published by the Linguistic Data Consortium at Penn (Strassel et al. 2003): Rose Barrise (Section 4), Adolphus Hester (Section 7), and Louise Atkins (Section 8).

They represent a series of stages in the research tradition that evolved beginning with my first project on Martha's Vineyard. The first speaker we encounter is Donald Poole, who was indeed the first person I interviewed there. The next two sections are on people I interviewed in 1963 on New York's Lower East Side: garment worker Rose Barrise (Section 4) and retired fireman Michael Duffy (Section 5). That study demonstrated how differences in the age, social class, and speech style of speakers were major factors in language variation, and that this variation could also be used to model the dynamics of language change.

The New York City project spawned similar research on a wide variety of languages in many places. Among studies of English were Trudgill (1974) in Norwich, United Kingdom; Shuy, Wolfram, and Riley (1967) in Detroit; Feagin (1979) in Anniston, Alabama. Early research projects on other languages included Gregersen and Pedersen (1991) on Danish; Naro (1981) and Scherre and Naro (1981) on Portuguese; Poplack (1989) on the bilingual French/English community of Canada's National Capital Region; and Sankoff and Cedergren (1971), D. Sankoff and G. Sankoff (1973), and G. Sankoff (2018) on French.

In the late 1960s, I began carrying out research designed to understand the patterns of change in vowel systems across the dialects of English. This research generated the interviews that are the focus of Sections 6 through 10, and were the basis for Labov, Yaeger, and Steiner (1972), later reported on in more detail in Labov (1994). The methods I used in these studies were further developed in my course Linguistics 560: "The Study of the Speech Community" and used by students in that course, taught between 1971 and 2015 at the University of Pennsylvania. Sections 11 and 12 present people interviewed by my students.

How did this assembly of life histories fall into the hands of students of the language, and where will it take us in our search for a deeper understanding of what people have to say? Perhaps we will learn what eloquence is. I hope so. But if not, we will rest content with having brought these great speakers to life.

At the start of the coronavirus pandemic in March 2020, Gillian and I were at home, like almost everyone else. Looking over the lists of the remarkable people interviewed over the years, the spreadsheet from our archive showed that I was registered as the interviewer for 1,006 subjects in the files. "How did you come to meet so many people?" she asked. "I don't know," I said. "It has something to do with what I was trying to find out about language and how it changes." "But from what you've told me, you were never Mr. Sociable when you were growing up," she said. I had to admit that she was right. How did I get so involved in the business of breaking the first rule that our parents give us: "Don't talk to strangers!"

To make any sense out of this story, I have to review my own linguistic history. Such a linguistic autobiography follows, with an account of who these strangers were talking to.

2 Growing Up in New Jersey

The story begins with a conversation in 1978. I had just been explaining myself to three young guys in New Mexico, and one of them said, "Just a minute. Do I understand that you go anywhere in the world that you want, and talk to people about anything you want to talk about?" I said, "Yeah, that's it." And he said, "I want that job."

I was not endowed by birth with the art of listening. If anything, I was a talker. I learned to listen by hanging out with people who were different from me, at the Union Ink Company, at Parris Island, and then with the 1,000 people who happened to be doing nothing else when I came around with my tape recorder.

My mother and my father grew up in the city of New Haven, Connecticut. My father studied chemistry at Yale and took his first job with Fuchs & Lang, a manufacturer of printing ink, in East Rutherford, New Jersey. In 1925, he and my mother moved to the town of Rutherford. My birth certificate shows that I was delivered in Passaic by the poet Dr. William Carlos Williams. At the peak of the Depression, my father set up his own business, the Union Ink Company, which eventually became highly specialized in silk screen inks.

The linguistic consequence of growing up in this corner of New Jersey was that I kept a comfortable distance from the linguistic self-hatred of New Yorkers that I described some thirty years later (Labov 1966). On the whole, I enjoyed the linguistic self-confidence that came with this distance from the City.

My father Benjamin Labov was equally at home with the English language. This is despite the fact that he was born in the city of Alexandria, in Ukraine. He came to the United States with his father Morris and mother Leah in 1906 at the age of nine, but followed the pattern of second-generation language loss that was so accurately documented by Joshua Fishman (Fishman 1966). The English of Rutherford was my mother tongue, as the English of New Haven was my father and mother's.[5] Not so for my father's brother Harry, three years older, a successful contractor in New Haven, who had a strong Yiddish accent to the day of his death.

I didn't have many friends in Rutherford. I was learning to be a listener, rather than a talker. My main contacts with working-class speakers were the kids of the Gusayef family who worked as janitors in the apartment house next door. Danny was a star discus thrower in the high-school team. Morris was a mean little kid who jumped on my back from behind.

I did learn another language: not Yiddish, but Hebrew. Every Monday through Thursday of the late 1930s, I strapped on my roller skates and made my way eastward across town, down through the business district and across the railroad tracks to the South Bergen Hebrew Institute, where I prepared myself to

---

[5] My mother used a fluent Yiddish with her parents. When I told her some of the things I had learned from my course on Yiddish dialectology with Uriel Weinreich, she said wistfully, "Billy, if you had only studied Yiddish!" But her mother tongue was Vilna Yiddish, in which she was fluent but not literate, and she never conceded that the standard language used the auxiliary *bin* in place of *hobm* in *Ich bin geboren* 'I was born'.

read the Torah and the Haftorah for my Bar Mitzvah. I learned to speak without understanding: religion was so much drudgery, and no less so to the Rebbe. He was a stout, aging individual enveloped in a yellowed tallis and equipped with the traditional Rebbe smell. I learned from him to respect the views of others no matter how far from my own: a quality that will be essential in this volume.

I remember the one time that I didn't: I addressed him on a question of doctrine. "Why," I said to him, "is God always asking us to tell him how good he is?" The rabbi was quite angry. He told me to concentrate on the tones and the gestures with which the Torah was delivered. But from that time on I had no confidence in the supernatural and its exponents. Science was more my style, though it was some time before I was able to get a handle on it.

My further contact with Hebrew (and Yiddish) came once a year at Passover when my family drove to New Haven to attend the Seder at my Uncle Harry's house. There was always quite a crowd of relatives present. At the head of the table were the older men, reading rapidly from well-worn copies of the Haggadah. The women of the household would be bustling in and out of the kitchen, getting ready for the evening meal, which was also a part of the ritual. The sounds of the Seder were blended with the sound of the elders pounding on the table in an appeal for the women to be quiet.

I don't remember any conversations with my grandparents. But when I taught an undergraduate course on narrative at Penn, I gave students the assignment of eliciting stories from their grandparents, with many remarkable results. It was not uncommon for them to say, "Why didn't they tell me this before?"

How many of us have had long conversations with our parents? In the old days, children were to be seen and not heard. Surely we have been scolded by them, instructed, and informed. In some families, dinner table conversations were a regular institution.[6] They might take the form of reports on how your day was. But if it was not easy to talk to our parents, it was no more likely that we would find ourselves in conversations with strangers. Many parents warned their children against such a thing.

The subject of this volume, conversations with strangers, is not a part of the daily life of most of us.

I got along well in my early school years at the Union Elementary and Junior High School, a red brick building just across the road from our house. I got used to being one of the smart kids, but my father took it out of me if I showed any tendency to think well of myself. Then he moved the Union Ink Company to Ridgefield, twenty miles closer to the big city, and I started the ninth grade in

---

[6] In many American families in the twenty-first century, the family dinner table itself has come to be a relic of the past (Ochs et al. 2011)

Fort Lee, at the New Jersey side of the George Washington Bridge. In Fort Lee High School I found myself in a permanent role as the leader of the smart kids, at the margins of the social life of the school – not someone who would engage freely in conversation with strangers.

Fort Lee was close to Manhattan in both language and cultural style. New York City was an important point of reference for everyone in Bergen County. Members of some families with close ties to New York had a strong City accent, where the final [r] in *car* was pronounced as "cah" and *card* as "cahd." But I kept my distance from New York, and maintained the [r] pronunciation in my own speech. The distance from New York City may have been helpful over the years, even when my main object was the sociolinguistic architecture of the metropolis.

In a remarkable parallel, sociolinguist Penny Eckert also grew up in a neighboring suburb of New York City: the middle-class town of Leonia, New Jersey. In her recent work (Eckert 2018), she describes her encounter with the accents and cultural style of the working-class high-school kids:

> In my own suburban adolescence in Leonia, New Jersey, I developed a strong local identity, neatly disciplined by my jocky participation in Leonia High School. But an important part of the local was Leonia's place in the broader suburban area, and particularly the suburb immediately to the south, Palisades Park, whose kids attended Leonia High School. When the kids from less affluent and largely Italian-American Palisades Park joined us in high school, class, ethnicity and geography came together, and Jersey phonology took on more meaning. I liked the fast Italian boys from Palisades Park, and I associated Jersey phonology with the things that made them preferable to the more vanilla Leonia boys – and with girls who snapped their gum and were less goody-goody than me. I associated Jersey phonology not just with social qualities but with the bodily styles that went with them – adornment, movement, posture, facial expressions, actions. Although Leonia and Palisades Park are contiguous in a vast suburban sprawl, we were all acutely aware of the boundary between the two towns. (Eckert 2018: 66–67)

Eckert was in the middle of things in high school, but as the next section makes plain, I was not. She was able to use her grasp of adolescent social structure to great advantage in her research in Detroit high schools (Eckert 1989).

2.1 Fort Lee High School and the Syndicate

Fort Lee was a divided community, largely working class, mainly Italian, German, and Polish. The majority of Fort Lee High School students, and the people I knew best, were from these families – some the closest of my friends, others in violent conflict, but when we met in later years we recognized a common ground. The southern portion of Fort Lee was called "Palisades," a population of upper middle-class homes that in our case justified the name by its location in the wooded cliffs that overlooked the Hudson River, and a more secluded house that was rumored to be inhabited by members of a Mafia family.

In my four years in Fort Lee High School I was an "A" student and a central member of a sophomoric group of six or seven non-conformists known locally as "The Syndicate." Included were some whose speech was, like mine, identified as "Jersey" and others who were heavily influenced by New York City speech. This latter group included my best friend Frank Scalpone, who has written to me that:

> The only thing about me that I can think of that may have won your attention
> as a youth was your mother's horror at my "New York" accent. She really
> wanted you to stop being friends with me. I tried to take this like a man.

There is no reason to think that Frank's accent interfered with his career in later life.[7] And we're still friends.

Syndicate members were neither Jocks nor Burnouts nor In-Betweens in the terminology of Eckert (1989), but did the minimum required to get good grades without participating in organized activities beyond that. Syndicate members were quite backward in their relations with the opposite sex. We also held aloof from any organization supported by the management: student government, theater, music, sports, dances, or what-have-you. What everybody did, we didn't do. Members went on to a wide variety of careers.

The Syndicate had nothing to do with the school paper, but we printed a six-page local newsletter variously connected with the Palisade (Manatuk) neighborhood, entitled: *The Manatuk Weekly and Literary Volcano and Bathroom Companion*.

In some ways, the school recognized the Syndicate as a part of its social fabric. The text beneath my picture in the Fort Lee High School yearbook read:

> William is our Syndicate Man.
> Try and beat him if you can.

When I fill out medical questionnaires these days, I write "never" under "Smoking," reflecting that the choice that protected my lungs was a product of non-conformity rather than intelligence. It seems that I had a lot to say but

---

[7] I recently wrote asking him to summarize his extraordinary career, which was in no way handicapped by his speech pattern. After an undergraduate degree at Fordham and several years studying English philology at Penn, he returned to New Jersey and became associate editor of a motor sport magazine, then Editor at *Boat Sport* magazine. After a decade as PR manager (and director of marketing) with Mercury, a major outboard motor company in Wisconsin, he was lured back to New York City to become manager of the National Boat Show.

I'm not sure what it was all about. The math teacher, Mrs. Quinn, once asked me, "William, why is it that when the students come into the classroom, I always hear your voice?"

2.2 Higher Education

Largely because my father and my older brother Richard had gone to Yale, I applied to Harvard in 1944, and "they let in anybody during the war." I lived in Adams House,[8] next to the Lampoon building, with many other eccentrics and radicals. My degree was in English and Philosophy. My freshman advisor was Professor John Wild, a Thomist philosopher. When he saw that my program included Chemistry B (Inorganic Chemistry), he said, "Where did you get this *idolatry* of science?" I was astonished. This was a very smart man. I *did* have an idolatry of science and still do, but how did he know? I studied composition with Harry Levin and I. A. Richards, Homeric Greek with Eric Havelock, and wrote a senior thesis on the concept of time in *Finnegan's Wake*.

All this was pretty far afield from the conversations with strangers that are the center of my concerns. But the connection was made when I got to know Murray Lerner, a member of the Harvard Film Club who eventually became an eminent documentary film maker. Murray was also to be my model in asking questions that captured the moving spirit of the times in the voices of people.

After graduating, I continued the radical politics of my college years, but without the caution needed in the commercial world. I lost one editorial position after marching in the May Day parade with the staff of Alfred A. Knopf and another when I left subscription lists for *The Daily Worker* on my desk at *Drug Trade News*. Fortunately, I had acquired enough chemistry in college to serve me well when I went to work in the laboratory of the family business: the Union Ink Company. There I learned to test my ideas about the real world against what the real world had to say. Would an ink dry fast enough to avoid offsetting on the page above it? Would it adhere to the latest plastic surface or survive the onset of snow and ice? The interaction with the material world went along with the change in the people I talked to in the factory or the shop. The people who held the floor were worth listening to.

A two-year break in this factory routine brought me into contact with a wider range of English speakers as the result of being drafted into the US Marine Corps during the Korean War. I spent the two years working on the Parris Island marine base while living in Beaufort, South Carolina. When I returned to work at Union Ink, I made printing inks and silk screen inks, in close association with the men of the factory. I was pretty good at it, and in fact I found that some of the inks I

---

[8] My daughter Jessie, who attended Harvard some forty years later, also lived in Adams House.

formulated were still in use in the industry forty years after I left the company. As much as I enjoyed this life, there were limitations to it. I found that there was less scope for my abilities than I would have liked. Some of the inks I had formulated were doing well. But there was no place in the trade journal for a paper on the properties of the new film-former. Those observations, together with the most recent formulas, were filed in an imaginary cabinet labeled "Trade Secrets."

When in 1961 it became increasingly clear that my own way of doing things had no future in the company, I took my leave and enrolled in graduate school at Columbia University to study – of all things – the changes taking place in the English language.[9] I had observed plenty of them in the speech of my factory friends, in the drafts passing through the Marine Corps base, and in the everyday speech of the silk screen printers. I read in the daily paper that these changes in English were outrageous, improper, and disgraceful, and I felt that someone should speak up for the working people I had come to know so well.

Linguistics was an attractive world of intense debate on the structure of language and its history of continual change. But I discovered that the activity was remote from the procedures I was used to in my laboratory work. Most of the linguists I met were gathering data by introspection, asking themselves, "Can I say this?" "Can I say that?" It occurred to me that I might start a new way of doing linguistics.

In this enterprise, I found that my years as an industrial chemist weren't wasted. I drew from them three assets. One was a firm conviction that the real world would prove you right or wrong when the products of your work were put to the test, perhaps by harsh weather, or under the pressure of high-speed printing presses. Second was that this result depended on a certain precision of method: you could never know if you were right or wrong unless you had entered in your notebook each step you had taken.[10] The third asset was a lasting acquaintance with working-class styles of speech – ways of arguing, joking, telling stories, and passing the time during the noon hour break. These were the elements that I put to work in a field that came to be called sociolinguistics, or later on, the study of linguistic change and variation.

To enter the study of linguistics at Columbia in 1961 was an incredible piece of good luck, in that my work was directly supervised by Uriel Weinreich – dialectologist, semanticist, Yiddishist, and general linguist. When I visited other

---

[9] The first class I took was an evening course on the history of English, with Allen Walker Read, who had authored a study of "OK" (Read 1963), and shown how much could be learned from the language of everyday life.

[10] When I was weighing out ingredients for an experimental mix in the laboratory, I was never sure that my father would not appear at my elbow: "What are you doing!!" And God help me if I hadn't written it down.

universities throughout the country, the mention of his name produced a look of respect that guaranteed me a hearing. The paper that we wrote with Marvin Herzog in 1967 (Weinreich, Labov, and Herzog 1968) has been the foundation of sociolinguistics, conveying Weinreich's world view to everyone who hopes to advance the study of language and language change.[11] When he died in 1967, no older than myself, I found in his papers a series of projects for the future of sociolinguistics that make it difficult to distinguish my own view of the field from his.

In 1970 I moved my base of operations to the University of Pennsylvania in Philadelphia and continued my studies of language change in that city. In the decades that followed, our archives of recorded speech grew to include all corners of the English-speaking world.

3 Martha's Vineyard, Massachussetts: Donald Poole, Fisherman

My first chance to test this new approach to linguistics was in 1961, on a visit to my Harvard friend Murray Lerner on the island of Martha's Vineyard, off the New England coast.[12] One of the first people I interviewed was recommended to me by Joseph Allen, the editor of the local newspaper. This was Donald Poole, an eighth-generation descendant of Yankee whalers and fishermen.[13]

In my interviews with Poole and other fishermen, farmers, local business owners, Yankees, Native Americans, and Portuguese, across three generations, I learned that the local people were under great pressure from the wealthy summer folks from the mainland, who were buying up as much desirable property as they could. Some younger people left the island but others stayed and resisted this outside pressure, and the particular sound change I was charting was strongest among them. Poole was one of the key figures in Chilmark, where the descendants of Yankee whalers were concentrated, and I was told that long-term summer people counted themselves as having arrived if Donald Poole said hello to them. He was also archetypical, for his generation, of the changes in speech sounds that I was studying.

---

[11] I have summarized the influence that paper had over the subsequent five decades (Labov 2020).

[12] The late filmmaker Murray Lerner was renting a modest summer house on the Vineyard. Murray was the creator of many films centering on music, beginning with Newport Folk Festival in the 1960s and the Isle of Wight Festival in 1969. He was the Oscar winner for *From Mao to Mozart* (1978). He interacts with many musicians in his films. Murray insisted that I use a professional-level tape recorder. I followed his advice in using the Nagra 1, 3, 4, and 4s in this and later recording. The quality of the speech sounds to be heard in this Element are a result of Murray's good counsel.

[13] An obituary for Donald Poole, who was born in 1905, appeared in the *Boston Globe* (August 1, 1984). It refers to him as "an authority on whaling and whale ships."

3.1 What Sounds Have to Say

I noticed that Vineyarders had a particular way of pronouncing words like *life, right, and rice* (with the diphthong *ay*); and *about*, *house*, and *couch* (with the diphthong *aw*).

Words like *about* and *life*, pronounced by Donald Poole:

Sound 1. Available at www.cambridge.org/conversationswithstrangers

about

Sound 2. Available at www.cambridge.org/conversationswithstrangers

life

In words like *about* (Sound 1) and *life* (Sound 2), the change involves the beginning vowel of the diphthong *a* ("ah") being pronounced higher in the mouth, or "centralized," eventually reaching the sound in *but* [bʌt]. This was particularly interesting because the *Linguistic Atlas of New England*, a generation before, had reported just the opposite (Kurath and McDavid 1963). The change was particularly strong in the up-island fishing village of Chilmark (population 200).

I traced the centralization of diphthongs across three generations of Vineyard families, taking into account gender, occupation, neighborhood, and ethnicity. My final conclusion was that what was driving this change was people's orientation toward the island: some people expressed positive attitudes to remaining on and working on the island; others were neutral; and a small number were negative, expressing a strong desire to leave. It goes without saying that Donald Poole was in the positive group.

For each speaker, the degree of centralization was measured on a four-point scale, and the average was calculated for each of three groups according to orientation toward the island. The end result was Table 1, which is taken from my paper "The social motivation of a sound change" (Labov 1963: 306).

A second factor showed that centralization was correlated with speakers' age: the younger the speaker, the higher the centralization value. This was the first quantitative study of sound change: each generation of speakers representing the language as it was when they acquired it. This second result revealed that an age distribution was an indication of language change.

When I delivered the paper to a full session of the Linguistic Society of America, I was prepared for considerable resistance, even decades of skeptical opposition. My romantic expectations were not fulfilled. The reverse was true: the linguists stood up to cheer. In the sixty years since, it has received a general approval that overrides partisan disputes as a model of how the relations of language to society are to be dealt with.

Table 1 Relation of centralization to orientation toward Martha's Vineyard

Number of persons	Orientation to the island	Mean centralization score for (ay)	Mean centralization score for (aw)
40	Positive	63	62
19	Neutral	32	42
6	Negative	09	08

As you will hear in the excerpts of his speech, Donald Poole was a leader in this sound change. And I became more and more immersed in what he was saying as well as how he was saying it. It was increasingly evident that his speech was a prototypical example of the sociolinguistic value of centralization.

3.2 The Man with a New England Conscience

It became clear that Donald Poole was more than a linguistic prototype: in my conversations with him, I was riveted by his powerful exposition of the Vineyarders' ideology. He was a prime advocate of the importance of work as a calling. One summer evening, I asked him about this (Sound 3).

Sound 3. Available at www.cambridge.org/conversationswithstrangers

WL: What reason do people have, to work harder than they have to, to earn a living?
DP: I can answer that for you 'cause I've already worked it out for myself and argued the point with a good many men. It's the satisfaction of feelin' that you have accomplished something over and above the bare necessities of life. You take a pride ... in doin' the best that you can according to your ability. I don't have to go fishin'. I can quit right now ... and be comfortable. But just as long as I draw the breath of life I'll be down in my boat in the mornin', at six or half past six in the mornin', bound somewhere, doin' all that I can, as best as I can, to the best of my ability and knowledge, because I take a pride in doing that, somethin' I know, and I feel that I'm doing something ... important. And I'm happier doin' that than I would be sittin' round to the beach. A man with a New England conscience can't sit still, and not produce something. As long as he has the ability to do it, and the knowledge of how to do it. Does that answer your question?
WL: Right down the line!

When I posed this question, I had in mind Weber's notion of the Protestant ethic (Weber 1948). Poole's answer resonated with me not only because it reverberated with the strong work ethic I had absorbed from my father. It was immediate, targeted, and powerful, extending to 261 words. He begins with a preface that claims that he has the answer, then defines that emotion involved and states clearly that there is satisfaction from its accomplishment.

There are a number of rhetorical elements in this response that account for its length and complexity. In Donald Poole's rhetoric, we recognize a New England preaching style, in which expressions of time, and human effort over time, are elaborated:

> "beyond what I need to live;"
> → *over and above the bare necessities of life*;
> "As long as I live"
> → *as long as I draw the breath of life*;
> "all that I can"
> → *all that I can, as best as I can, to the best of my ability and knowledge*

His convictions about the importance of work are strikingly evident when we hear the final words of his response – "A man with a New England conscience can't sit still" – and his challenge to me to agree with him: "Does that answer your question?"

I was taken aback. Concepts that I had absorbed in the lectures of an historian now reached me in the words of a New England fisherman.[14] As I listened again to this passage, I found that it exemplifies the highly structured character of Poole's prose. In the sentence that begins with "As long as I draw the breath of life," the causal structure is elaborated to three levels of subordination. The first, temporal clause is followed by the main clause. Next comes a locative clause and two manner clauses that modify it, indicating how "being down in his boat in the morning" will be accomplished. Finally, there are a further three clauses that give the reasons why Poole will be down in his boat in the morning.

3.3 Happiness

For further examples of Poole's rhetoric, we may look to his response to another of my general questions, on the nature of happiness, which ultimately links to work (Sound 4). Near the beginning of this excerpt, we again hear the centralization of (ay) in the phrase "a successful life". The Nagra recorder also faithfully transmits the voices of the crickets.

Sound 4. Available at www.cambridge.org/conversationswithstrangers

---

[14] Only two years earlier, Perry Miller, one of my Harvard professors of history, had written an article with the title: "The New England Conscience" (Miller 1958–59).

WL: Would you care to define that? What is happiness?

DP: Oh, that's very easy young man. That's very easy indeed. I've thought about this very deeply and my wife and I have discussed it a great deal. A lot depends in the first place how you define success. Happiness and success should go together. And what is a, a successful life, to me, may not be to you. But I believe, and I live, the theory, that a man can be the most successful and also the most happy, if he's doing the type of work which he enjoys. Every day's work is not work, it's not really a challenge, but it's a pleasure, to do somethin' that you enjoy doin' and you feel that you know something about and that you can continue to learn something about. In other words it's a – If I can make it clear to you, happiness consists mostly, other things being equal, of having the ability, when you go to bed at night, think back about what you have done during the day, to feel that you have accomplished something useful. I brush aside the, the point that you must provide for your family, which we're all supposed to do. That uh, perhaps that can – perhaps, yes I'm sure, that enters into happiness. But uh, a man has to live with himself. And nobody knows himself like he does. What goes through your mind in the course of a day. If you go to bed at night, and you feel more or less satisfied and contented that you've done the best you could, you've been fairly successful that things have turned out well for you durin' the day, what's wrong with that? Isn't that happiness?

Poole didn't let my lack of experience interfere with learning more about Vineyard ways of doing and dealing with the world. He invited me to a day fishing on his boat and was not surprised when the smell of the shrimp bait made me seasick. I was also invited to dinner at his house, to sample Mrs. Poole's "Brown Betty" dessert. I didn't have my tape recorder, but I was thoughtless enough to ask him a question at the end of the meal. "Mr. Poole," I said, "what is a Yankee?" Poole was silent for a good twenty seconds, and then he said, "There are twenty things that make up a Yankee, and the first is the fear of a living God." I tried desperately to remember what followed, but all I have left is that.

3.4 Eloquence

Our examination of the speech of Donald Poole began with the study of his phonetics – the sound pattern of *right*, *life*, etc. But my interest in his sound pattern eventually gave way to a search for the sources of his eloquence and the larger question: what are the sources of eloquence among our speakers of English? The standard dictionary definitions (Oxford English Dictionary; Merriam-Webster) look to a combination of two properties: *force*, which is largely related to *authority*, and *persuasiveness*. The force of Poole's rhetoric is a product of his reputation and his formulation: the most eloquent sentences combine between six and eight clauses.

Eloquence may take many forms, and the ten speakers who appear here use a variety of rhetorical strategies. As we go on, the many different linguistic forms used by these strangers will expand our knowledge of what language can be like.

Donald Poole was not an isolated voice in the community, but a powerful exponent of community sentiment, which can be understood as one of the forces that move the language. As Eckert later expressed it, "The Martha's Vineyard fishermen, in appropriating the centralized variant of (ay), were not simply claiming to be Vineyarders but were making a claim about what a Vineyarder is" (Eckert 2018: 155.) Eckert's statement coincides very well with what Donald Poole has to say on the matter (Sound 5):

Sound 5. Available at www.cambridge.org/conversationswithstrangers

> You see, you people who come down here to Martha's Vineyard don't understand the background of the old families on the island. Strictly maritime background and tradition. Our interests run that way, our thoughts still run that way, I'm speaking now of the descendants of the old families. Now what we're interested in, the rest of America, this part over here across the water that belongs to you and we don't have anything to do with, has forgotten all about the maritime tradition and the fact that if it hadn't been for the interest that the early settlers in this country took in the ocean, both as whalemen, as fisherman, and as seamen and merchant sailors, this country couldn't have existed, the Plymouth Colony would've been a failure.

The rest of this volume will deal with remarkable individuals as eloquent in their use of the English language as is Donald Poole. The central figures in each section will share their eloquence. They have much to tell us if we listen. We will find that the social meanings of the sound patterns we have studied are expressed even more clearly in the broader rhetoric of our gifted speakers.

Stephen Spielberg's movie *Jaws* was filmed on Martha's Vineyard, and Donald Poole, playing the harbormaster, appears in one scene walking across the Menemsha dock. We learn from a post by his son, Everett Poole, that Spielberg spent every lunchtime talking with Everett's father in his truck.

> My father, Donald Poole, played the Amity harbormaster. Although they served a full-blown lunch on the set every day, the old man took his dinner pail with him so he could sit in his pickup truck with his dog and have his regular lunch. There was a young guy who'd come over after he got his lunch

from the cafeteria line and eat with the old man in the truck. He'd sit and ask him all kinds of questions about fishing and the Island. They did this day after day. One day the old man asked my wife [Assistant Location Casting Director, Jini Poole], "Who's that young guy who sits in the truck and has lunch with me every day? He's a very nice fellow, and I have a good time talking to him." Jini said, "That's Steve Spielberg!" And so my father wound up having a very good relationship with the director without even knowing who he was! (Everett Poole in Wainfur 2012)

I had long thought that the quantitative analysis in my 1963 paper was the source of its acclaim, but I now realize that the effect of Donald Poole's rhetoric on me was what has kept me coming back to him. We have to admit that certain individuals can epitomize a community. Stephen Spielberg obviously agreed with my appreciation of Donald Poole.

4 New York City, New York: Rose Barrise, Garment Worker

The language that I recorded on Martha's Vineyard was not well known to my readers: their voices resonated in farms and villages of several hundred. But the next study I undertook had to deal with a stereotype that could not have been embedded more deeply in American folklore: the English of New York City. I was then enrolled in Linguistics at Columbia University. I took a course with Herbert Hyman in the Sociology Department and learned the basic techniques of survey methodology. This did not involve introductions to strangers, but rather an enumeration of all of the dwelling units in the area and the random selection of individuals to represent the community. My research on the Lower East Side was a "piggyback study," a subset of the subjects of the "Delinquency and Opportunity" survey by the Bureau of Applied Social Research (Cloward and Ohlin 1960). I mailed a letter from the "American Language Survey" to 189 of the New Yorkers who had been selected for the sociology survey, and 122 people responded positively when I knocked on their doors.[15] Most of them did not remember getting the letter, and I was a stranger to them when I appeared on the doorstep.

4.1 The Stranger at the Door

Rose Barrise lived in an apartment on the Lower East Side, only two blocks from the factory where she worked. When I approached the building, I didn't realize that the tape recorder was on, so the first sounds on the recording are my footsteps on the stairway (Sound 6).

---

[15] Most of those who were not interviewed were people who were not home (Labov 1966 [2006]: Appendix D).

Sound 6. Available at www.cambridge.org/conversationswithstrangers

> [footsteps, knocking]
> WL: Hello!! [sound of door opening]
> WL: Mrs. Barrise?
> RB: Yeah?
> WL: My name is Labov, from the American Language Survey. We wrote you a letter, oh, a couple of weeks back I think.
> RB: About what?
> WL: Well, our business is the American language, the way people talk. We travel across the country, from place to place, and uh, finding out the differences between the way people talk from one area to another! For example, well, I think you, you may remember, you must've gotten a letter from us.
> RB: I don't remember.

My attempts at an explanation proceeded for a few minutes until she burst out impatiently (Sound 7):

Sound 7. Available at www.cambridge.org/conversationswithstrangers

> RB: Now tell me! What is the idea? I wanna know about this!
> WL: OK.
> RB: Explain yourself!

For another forty-five seconds, I tried again to explain the purpose of the project until she interrupted once more (Sound 8):

Sound 8. Available at www.cambridge.org/conversationswithstrangers

> RB: Yeah! But who's puttin' out this, uh,
> WL: Oh, well I'm from Columbia University, I'm in the Department of Languages there, that's my business.

The mention of Columbia University carried weight. With her concerns resolved, Barrise proved to be a voluble talker and a warm and welcoming person, generous in sharing her ideas and experiences. She addressed me as "Bill" over coffee and cake with her husband and son, whom I interviewed later on. She was a native-born New Yorker; her parents were Italian immigrants. Barrise had had to leave school after the 6th grade. At the age of forty-three, she had been a factory worker for almost three decades.

4.2 New York City Speech

Much of the interview concerned language and language differences. Like all other New Yorkers, Barrise looked down on the speech of her own city. "What do you think about Mayor Wagner's speech?" "Terrible!" "And Governor Rockefeller?" "I don't like it either." Her own speech matched the "r-less" pattern of the New Yorkers that I studied in the 1960s. In the casual speech of everyday life, New Yorkers variably pronounced *r* that occurs after a vowel unless it was followed by a vowel – words like *car* and *card* were pronounced as "cah" and "cahd." In casual speech, the great majority of New Yorkers pronounced *r* as a consonant only 5 percent of the time in words like this (Labov 1966 [2006]: 151). Dividing all the speakers of my 1963 survey into nine socially stratified levels, only those in the upper middle class pronounced it as a consonant more frequently, and then only 20 percent of the time. Barrise's rate in this interview, 5 percent, matched that of the great majority of New Yorkers at that time.[16]

As a way of verifying that this pattern was not restricted to residents of the Lower East Side, I undertook a "rapid and anonymous" survey to extend my study of New Yorkers from the Lower East Side to another group of strangers: the 264 employees of three New York City department stores. The linguistic variable of interest was the pronunciation of *r* as either "vocalized" (sounding like a vowel) or pronounced as a consonant. The Lower East Side study had shown the consonantal pronunciation to be socially stratified – much more frequent among speakers who were upper middle or upper class. Although in terms of a simple occupational scale, department store employees might be considered to be in the same bracket, working conditions in the three stores meant that their employees were also socially stratified in the order of prestige of the stores: Saks > Macy's > S. Klein (Labov 1966 [2006]: 46). A "rapid and anonymous" study takes advantage of "free goods" (Goffman 1983: 37) – e.g. asking for the time, or for directions to some location. In each store, I asked the employees for a location that I knew was on the *fourth floor* – women's shoes, in the case of Saks. In each case, I asked a second time, and then went off in the direction indicated. I then noted down whether or not the *r* in these two words was pronounced as a consonant, along with the person's sex, approximate age, and particular occupation (stocker, manager, etc.). Each employee thus had four opportunities to pronounce *r* as a consonant. In Saks, 30 percent of the sixty-eight employees did so, but the rate in Macy's was lower: only 20

---

[16] In a sequence like *far and wide* or associated with a mid vowel (as in *first*). Barrise follows closely the pattern of this variation described in Labov (1966 [2006]).

percent (N=125). In S. Klein's, only three of the seventy-one employees I spoke to pronounced all four *r*s as a consonant, a rate of 4 percent, and fifty-six of them registered no consonantal *r* at all. The Department Store study also confirmed the greater use of consonantal *r* among younger speakers – a change that has been traced across many decades in subsequent research [Fowler 1986; Becker 2009, 2010; Newman 2014]. Fowler repeated the Department Store study some twenty years later, substituting May's for S. Klein (which had closed in the meantime). The same social stratification was observed, as well as an overall increase in consonantal *r* over the two decades.

When Barrise discovered that the interview would deal with language, she raised an issue she had been wondering about: the difference between her own New York City speech and that of people in New Jersey where her family had a summer cottage (Sound 9). A linguistic feature of interest is the treatment of final *t*. Barrise's New York City dialect variably includes the use of a strongly released final *t*. In the following segment, we hear it in her second use of the word *accent*, and the *that* that follows it. Here we see that final *t* carries systematic social information of another type: for Barrise, a strongly released *t* appears (variably) in her most emphatic statements, which may link NYC speech to its use in other dialects as a stylistic resource (Eckert 2000: 128–29). Michael Newman (2014) summarizes the research of four authors who consider it to be "a marker of Jewishness" but observes himself that strongly released [t]'s before a pause are "widespread in New York among Jews and non-Jews alike" (85), particularly among "White New Yorkers" (84). He notes its use by politicians: Mayor Ed Koch, Governor Andrew Cuomo, and Senator Bernie Sanders.

Sound 9. Available at www.cambridge.org/conversationswithstrangers

> Yeah. In New Jersey, why is it that they have a certain kind of an accent? But an accent, that uh, they have a drawl.

4.3 Talking to Strangers

In this study of the Lower East Side, Rose Barrise gives us a clear model of urban working-class life and language. But she also displays a remarkable example of urban–rural interaction. Her reflections on the speech and customs of New Jersey are based on the time she has spent in the country town of Newton,[17] near the Delaware Water Gap, where her family planned to retire. Only fifty-five miles from her home on Cherry Street in the Lower East Side, it

---

[17] In 1960, the population of Newton was just over 6,500 (Newton, New Jersey – Wikipedia, en.wikipedia.org, accessed 9/13/2021).

is a world apart. Barrise gives a detailed account of walking along the road with her little niece, when she violated the basic parental rule: don't talk to strangers.

Barrise explains that people in the country, where the houses are very far apart, typically offer a lift to people they don't know (Sound 10). The vocalization of *r* in this segment can be heard in "over there."

Sound 10. Available at www.cambridge.org/conversationswithstrangers

> They uh, for instance if we're walking down the road, and uh, you know, over there it's a mile, a mile apart, you find another house, maybe another two miles, and uh, even if they don't know you, they can be complete strangers, they ask if you want a lift. On friendly basis! Some of them have families, and they even squeeze more people in, if you wanna go, how far you wanna go.

She continues by recounting what actually happened, expressing some doubt about accepting a ride (Sound 11).

Sound 11. Available at www.cambridge.org/conversationswithstrangers

> So once I, I agreed upon it, I says, "I wonder if I should take a chance, you don't have to be afraid." And me and my little niece I had with me, they took us a mile away from my house, to Five Points.

The strangers were kind enough to take them exactly where they wanted to go (Sound 12).

Sound 12. Available at www.cambridge.org/conversationswithstrangers

> And that's where my cousin lived! And they dropped us right off that corner and on their merry way they went.

Readers of this account may find themselves puzzled by the expression "on their merry way they went." What does she mean by "on their merry way"? There is some room for misinterpretation here. At first glance, it is an appreciative comment that reinforces the solidarity of country and city people. But the ambiguity of "on their merry way" throws doubt upon this interpretation. The Oxford English Dictionary defines *(on) one's merry way* as "to continue heedlessly, to proceed regardless of the consequences." Merriam-Webster notes that it is "often disapproving: to continue doing what one has been doing," citing the example: "She just goes on her merry way, loving men and then breaking their hearts." Barrise is apparently not entirely at ease with her country neighbors, when she decides to tell her niece that it is okay to talk to strangers in this case. Though she has told her niece that it is all right, she's not so sure herself.

I found myself reacting with admiration for Barrise's rhetorical range in this friendly interaction. The pronunciation of *ask* as *aks* is a vernacular feature, whereas the stylistic inversion in "On their merry way they went" echoes literary formality in putting "on their merry way" at the beginning of the sentence. *Went* is emphatic, with its strongly released final t perhaps signaling the end of that episode. A quantitative study of any one of these might place her in the social class system, but their combination is the work of a conversational artist.

4.4 A Leader of Language Change

The New York City study (Labov 1966 [2006]) was the first to firmly establish a finding that went against the popular view that blames language change on uneducated speakers, or praises changes that originate in a social or literary elite. Rather, the leaders of change were found to be neither at the top nor at the bottom of the social ladder. The daughter of Italian immigrants, Rose had had to leave school and go to work at the age of fourteen, but had become a forewoman in the factory, proud of her sewing skills and expertise. She and her husband had been able to buy a car, and looked forward to a secure retirement with a cottage in the country. In the analysis of phonological change in the New York City data, lower middle- and upper working-class speakers like Barrise were found to be in the lead. She was also a leader in a change that I had not examined at that time, the use of the verb "go" to introduce quoted speech. In a later paper, "The role of the avant garde in linguistic diffusion" (Labov 2018), I noted that the first wave of this innovation was among people born in the 1930s. Barrise, born in 1920, was clearly a member of the avant garde in using quotative "go" (Sound 13).

Sound 13. Available at www.cambridge.org/conversationswithstrangers

WL: When the car was turning over, what did you think?
RB: It was upside down. You know what happened? Do you know how I felt? I don't remember anything, this is really the truth, till today I could tell that to anybody, and they don't believe me, they'd think I'm kiddin' you. All I remember is, I thought I fell asleep. And I was in a dream. I actually saw stars, you know, stars in the sky, you know when, you look up there, and I was seein' stars, and then after a while, I felt somebody, pushing, piling, you know they were all on top of each other, and they were pullin' us out from the bottom of the car, and I was goin' "Ooh!" and when I came, y'know, to, I says to myself, "Ooh, we were in a car accident." And that's all I remember.

In describing her feelings when she came to after the car accident, we hear Barrise using both *go* and *say*: *I was **goin'** "Ooh"*; and *I **says** to myself, "Ooh,* *we were in a car accident.*" In other passages cited here, she again alternates between *go* and *say.*

- *they listen to me, they go, "Oh gee, it is,"*
- *when I try to help a person they go, "Oh please don't try and tell me"*
- *I says, "I wonder if I should take a chance"*

4.5 Common Sense

Like many other second-generation Americans, Rose Barrise found employment as a skilled worker in New York's garment industry. At the time of the Lower East Side interviews, she found herself in daily contact with younger women of less experience, largely Black and Puerto Rican. Her dealings with the younger generation are foregrounded in the section of the interview dealing with common sense (Sound 14).

Sound 14. Available at www.cambridge.org/conversationswithstrangers

WL: Well what does common sense mean to you?
RB: Common sense is saying the right words or the right conversation at the right time, and the appropriate time.

Although she accords this ability to everyone, she argues that the girls at work don't always use it (Sound 15).

Sound 15. Available at www.cambridge.org/conversationswithstrangers

> I mean they all have common sense, but sometimes they say something or they do something where they're not usin' their common sense at that time or at that moment.

Readers familiar with how frequently disagreements are generated in the workplace will be impressed as I was by Barrise's portrait of the relationship between old hands and newcomers on the job (Sounds 16 and 17).

Sound 16. Available at www.cambridge.org/conversationswithstrangers

> And, and it annoys me, because when I try to explain, or show them something, like up my shop, you know, because I've been working since I was a little girl, and I know, I can, I know, y'know we work on sportwear, and I could do anything, almost even with my eyes closed, and when I try to help a person they go, "Oh please don't try and tell me, I know how to do it this way," but they're doin' it wrong, and they have a pride, and they're not usin' their common sense, meanwhile they're doin' up their garment wrong, and before you know it they're bringin' all the work back at them, and they have to rip it.

Sound 17. Available at www.cambridge.org/conversationswithstrangers

> And some of them, they, they listen to me, they go, "Oh gee, it is," I sez "This is a shortcut, and it's easier," for them, and they can remember, and they could easily concentrate on it.

In these memorable interviews with Rose Barrise, she projects a vivid view of human interaction among a wide range of New Yorkers. She makes us wish that her capacity for dealing with others was more widely shared among members of the speech community.

5 New York City, New York: Michael Duffy, Fireman

Among the first interviews I did on the Lower East Side was one in September 1963 with Michael Duffy, a short, white-haired man of seventy-one, who was a voluble representative of New York City's Irish working class. He was a force to be reckoned with in the boxing ring, but had also worked as a truck driver, a policeman, a soldier, and a fireman. In listening to him, we learn a great deal about the struggles, techniques, and achievements of someone who has devoted his working life to saving the lives of others. From his first words, we hear the authentic New Yorker who grew up in the decade before the First World War. Like Barrise, he vocalizes *r* before vowels 95 percent of the time, but unlike Barrise, we hear from him the most traditional marker of New York City speech in the pronunciation of "first" (Sound 18):

Sound 18. Available at www.cambridge.org/conversationswithstrangers

The Penn Sociolinguistic Archive contains dozens of records of interviews I did with firemen, with increasing frequency over the years. The initial motivation for interviewing firemen was that they are a well-defined working group who – waiting for the next call – have time on their hands.

Duffy was in fact recruited into both the police and the fire departments. Although he had only two years of schooling, he managed to teach himself to read, enough to pass examinations for both departments. We will see that Duffy has a great deal to say on every subject. He speaks, moreover, as an irascible Irishman, with a high pitched, explosive style which challenges you to disagree with him. Conversation with Duffy is not a series of exchanges, but rather a series of corrections and denunciations.

Near the beginning of most interviews, I asked about education, and soon discovered that many of the older people who had had very little schooling were embarrassed by it. Asking them "How many years of schooling did you get a chance to finish?" was a way to alleviate embarrassment, and resonate with the circumstances of their upbringing (Sound 19).

Sound 19. Available at www.cambridge.org/conversationswithstrangers

WL: Where did you go to school?

MD: Public school!!

WL: Public school? And how many years of school did you get a chance to finish?

MD: Oh them days, I guess every – we're speakin' about two years. I was a great advocate of readin' signs, that's where I learned everything I ever learned.

WL: So when you, in other words when you first went out to uh, to work, you really didn't have any schooling at all.

MD: Not what you'd term an education! No, in no respects!!

Duffy's first career was interrupted by World War I. In explaining how he was recruited, instead of saying "I was called up," he personifies the army in the shape of an invitation from Uncle Sam (Sound 20).

Sound 20. Available at www.cambridge.org/conversationswithstrangers

MD: So I took the examinations and I passed with flying colors!!

WL: So you became a- which one? A policeman or a fireman?

MD: I become a, – first I become a policeman! So I took the job! I was on there about a year and a half, and Uncle Sam, says "Come on over and see what you can do on the other side for a while. It's gettin' tough over there!" I went over there for 18 months! In the meantime I was appointed to the fire department! So while I was there, maybe you shouldn't put this in, my sister sent me a letter, she says, in Belgium, "What will we do with these checks?" Not check – CHECKS! She said "We're gettin' CHECKS every month from the police and fire!" So I wrote back. I was in the machine gun company, "SPEND 'EM AS FAST AS YOU GET 'EM. I MAY NOT BE BACK!" See it shows you what kind of records, see? I was appointed a fireman shortly after I was drafted! I don't – what the hell, the way they kept records I don't know, they both sent CHECKS!

The two jobs he held at the same time were only one aspect of his dual identity. As with those who knew him, we are entitled to ask who we are dealing with, Duffy or Duffin, the name of everyone else in his family (Sound 21).

Sound 21. Available at www.cambridge.org/conversationswithstrangers

WL: Duffin!

MD: The priest was drunk when he baptized me! And I never bothered about it. I went down to get me baptism, pay for the job in the fire department. And the cop he says, "Your name is Duffy. The priest that baptized you is dead 20 years. But it's still Duffy!" I went to war, went to the fire department, came back, went to the Todd shipyard, the hell with it, I'm Duffy. But I'm the only one in the family, Duffy! I never changed it!

5.1 Strangers in the Ring

The question of who Duffy is is even more pressing when we are introduced to his fifth career (subsequent to being a horse-drawn wagon driver, a policeman, a fireman, and a gunner) as an amateur boxer. When the local favorite offers to fight "anybody in the house," Duffy is ready (Sound 22).

Sound 22. Available at www.cambridge.org/conversationswithstrangers

WL: All right you go to a, a big meeting, and did you know that somebody wasn't going to show up?

MD: No! We'd just take them chances! I never really, what you call 'em, had a manager! We'd just go to a fight.

WL: So the guy would say, uh,

MD: So-and-so's unable to appear, his opponent broke his leg or … fell in front of a car or some goddam thing. But to make good they'd fight anybody in the house! That was a tough expression in them days.

WL: So you'd go up there and –

MD: And, the house br- tout would say "We got a man!"

Who is Michael Duffy? A further challenge from Dick McGee, and Duffy launches into a dramatic narrative, ending up with his opponent's supporters pelting him with bottles (Sound 23).

Sound 23. Available at www.cambridge.org/conversationswithstrangers

So we're goin' along and I– he says to me, Dick McGee. We're strangers. He said, "I don't know your work." None of us are gettin' nuttn' for it. First of all, "Take it easy!" I said, "It's fine Dick!" "Who are you?" I said, "What's the difference? I'm doin' this for a fella just like yourself." So sure enough, out we go in the first round, Dick hits me, I seen everybody dead belongin' to me! But I shook it off, I was young, I come back there in the corner and the guy says to me, "Watch it, he's tryin' to knock you out!" I said, "No kiddin." Of course they can see better than us, you know. I said, "You serious?" He said "Yeah, he's tryin' to put you away." So I go out in the second round and he makes a mistake and bang! Down goes Dick in a heap. And Dick STAYS down, he don't get up, I said "I killed him!" Every bottle come at me in the regiment!

Donald Poole and Rose Barrise use fronting as part of their rhetorical repertoire. In this passage, Michael Duffy also uses this syntactic option to good effect. He might have started his account by saying "we went out in the first round". Instead, he starts with three rhetorical choices that heighten the drama, saying "So sure enough, out we go in the first round." *Sure enough* sets the listener up for the initial failure he is about to present; the drama is increased by using the historical present; and he fronts the adverbial phrase *out we go*.

Duffy is also a retired fireman, with twenty-five years of experience on the job. The largest part of his interview is devoted to how the people involved – residents, firemen, officers – deal with each other and with matters of life and death in the burning buildings. The interviewer is interested, for he seldom gets a chance to penetrate so deeply into the structure of these buildings. In no other occupation does so much rest on the decision to turn left or right, to go down to the cellar or up to the roof (Sound 24).

Sound 24. Available at www.cambridge.org/conversationswithstrangers

> Well you'd see a cellar and smoke was comin' up, pourin', flames and everything else. Well you'd deliberately see a fireman slide down there on their ass, down that cellar. When they got down there they could play pinochle.[18]

But the roof is the other way around. Duffy explains that this is because the gas, heat, and fumes rise (Sound 25).

Sound 25. Available at www.cambridge.org/conversationswithstrangers

> And even an, an interior stairway, that you come in this hallway and go down that cellar here, we gotta open up the door. And the sole reason why they send two firemen up the next building to break the fan light. If they didn't uh, bust that fan light on the roof, uh skylight, you couldn't make them stairs, firemen or nobody couldn't make it. Because the back draft would collect and take the firemen right up and throw 'em out in the street like flies.

5.2 Duffy's Work Ethic

Donald Poole intends to work "as long as I draw the breath of life"; Michael Duffy asserts that he will work "till the day they throw dirt in me face." He says

---

[18] The classic German card game pinochle was a favorite among firemen.

he wants "to be found dead on a truck." And like Poole, he has arranged his
finances so that he does not need to work. I mentioned to him that he must be
long retired (Sound 26):

Sound 26. Available at www.cambridge.org/conversationswithstrangers

MD: Since 1942! They don't owe me nothin', and I'm still goin', I'm drivin'a
truck every day. A two and a half ton truck. From the fire department, I get
$2600. And I get me full social security too. But I'm working for my brother.

Though Poole and Duffy are both exceptionally fluent and powerful
speakers, and masters of English idiom from their own range of experience,
they are sharply differentiated in their use of the standard social class linguistic variables, as well as in their social class and generation. Poole was a high
school graduate, and Duffy had only two years of schooling. Poole was an
entrepreneur who owned his own boat, while Duffy was solidly anchored in
the upper working class as fireman, policeman, and driver. Poole's usage was
consistently standard, while Duffy's was consistently marked by double
negatives.[19]

5.3 The Logic of Double Negatives

The use of double negatives is a prominent and perfectly regular feature of the
grammar of working-class English (Labov 1966 [2006]). In such sentences, a
single negative (*not, don't, didn't, never*, etc.) is followed by a second negation:
no, none, nobody, nothin', and so on. In an interview of ninety minutes, Duffy's
rate of double negatives is 100 percent (15/15). The following list will show the
commitment to double negatives in Duffy's rhetoric. Given Duffy's emphatic
style, one is torn between interpreting double negation as a social class marker
and as a component of a belligerent discourse. You may want to compare your
own capacity for strengthening negation with that of Michael Duffy.

1. I don't want no police job, forget about it, 25 dollars a week?
2. I dunno whether I want to be a fireman or a cop, I don't wanna be nothin', I
   guess.
3. They don't owe me nothin', and I'm still goin'.
4. He gives me 20, 25 bucks, it don't make no difference.
5. Well, none of us are gettin' nuttn'.
6. Oh yeah. You didn't fight, you wouldn't get no pay.
7. I never got nuttin.'

---

[19] We note that Duffy's description of the technical details of firefighting is in no way hampered by
non-standard English features like *them stairs* or the use of words like *bust (that fanlight)*.

8. That doesn't make no difference, you gotta fight him!
9. I never did no fishing.
10. No reason for nobody to get hurt!
11. You couldn't make them stairs, firemen or nobody couldn't make it.
12. You could have a couch smoldering there for hours, and didn't get no air and didn't start up yet.
13. They don't wanna go in no place that they know they're not sure of gettin' out of.
14. You didn't need your wife's consent or nobody's.
15. It don't make no difference.

We have seen that Michael Duffy is a master of many trades. Not the least of his skills is his mastery of the English language, which he uses to inform, to rebuke, to amuse, and to improve our chances of survival if events should turn out that way.

6 Rural Pennsylvania: Bill Peters, Farmer

I met the next in this set of strangers in 1969, when I was engaged in a series of exploratory studies to find out how far the Philadelphia vowel system extended to the west. I was driving through the small town of Duncannon, near the state capital of Harrisburg. There I met a member of the older generation who rivaled Michael Duffy in his belligerent use of the English language. Bill Peters was a white-haired, elderly man sitting on the porch of a grey-shingled farm house. There was nothing in his manner or appearance that would lead me to think that he was a rhetorician of a high order. I introduced myself as someone interested in the changes that were taking place in the region, and asked if I could sit down and talk with him.

I asked him about his early schooling (Sound 27). After a start in different schools, he returned to Duncannon, but his school days were limited. From an early age, he defied authority, challenging the school directors, who objected to his decision to quit.

Sound 27. Available at www.cambridge.org/conversationswithstrangers

> Then, I come back in to Lower Duncannon Penn Township, and I went to school there till I was about 12 or 13, and then I quit. And uh, the directors wasn't satisfied with that. They called me in, of course my dad was taking me in, and give me an examination.

Like Michael Duffy, Peters had very little schooling, but in applying to quit school, he bested the examiners, who had made the mistake of asking him an arithmetic question (Sound 28).

Sound 28. Available at www.cambridge.org/conversationswithstrangers

> And they shouldn't have given me that, because I was so canny with arith-
> metic it wasn't funny. But they didn' know that! The teacher did and I did, of
> course. I done that and they said, "Well then, I guess if he wants to quit school,
> why he can."

6.1 The Modern World

In answer to my question about what has changed since he was young, Peters
quickly turned to MONEY. As he thinks about it, his voice gains strength and
volume (Sound 29).

Sound 29. Available at www.cambridge.org/conversationswithstrangers

BP: Oh well ... in that time, if you wanted to go someplace, you walked! If you
had a horse you drove a horse. Now then, you just step outside the door and you
get in the car and you go where you want to and come when you please, I guess.
And you're payin' money for it every time you step on that gas. And you don't
keep a car only a year or so. You buy a new one, because you can go down an' get
the money outa'th'bank, or in – And, let the man take his car in, pay 'at 'un off 'n'
get a new one, an' you drive a new one.
WL: Well,
BP: Money's cheap, you can get – everybody has gobs and gobs of money! I
said gobs, and I know they have gobs of it. Because I attend the sales now
and then. And there's no limit to the money! Ev-everybody, every KID has
got money, every woman has got money, whether she's old or young, she's
got it. 'N' every man's got money.

6.2 Independence

But it turned out that the central theme of Peters' life was not money, but
independence. At this point in the interview, I asked him a question that has
produced remarkable answers from many people (Sound 30). Throughout the
interview, Peters combines a deliberate, measured rhythm of delivery with a
mastery of syntax that allows him to pronounce himself with multiply embedded clauses. No one has soared to the heights of eloquence that we hear from
Bill Peters.

Sound 30. Available at www.cambridge.org/conversationswithstrangers

WL: Is there one thing that happened to you that sticks in your mind, that you'd never forget, if there was one thing, one time, something that happened, what would that be?

BP: I'll answer it like this. If I was twenty years old, and know when I was twenty what I know now, I wouldn't marry the best woman, that ever walked in shoe leather, if she had a trillion o' money, and said "Bill, this is yours." "Honey, I don't want you." I would never marry another woman under the sun. If she could keep me and I'd never need to do a thing. I'd wanna work myself, the way I wanna work, go out and get a job, do what I wanna, come when I please, and have no obligation, only for myself.

The sentence that begins "if I was twenty years old" starts with a complex set of conditional clauses: "If I was twenty years old, and know when I was twenty what I know now." These precede the main clause: "I wouldn't marry the best woman" and its accompanying relative clause: "that ever walked in shoe leather." The sentence ends with another conditional: "if she had a trillion of money and said, 'Bill, this is yours.'" It concludes with an emphatic negative: "Honey, I don't want you." Seamlessly and spontaneously produced, it is followed by a further denial and an assertion of the value freedom has for Peters.

Peters makes it clear that he is not a misogynist; he concludes he had "a helluva good woman, don't get me wrong." Rather, a lifetime of experience has taught him that his highest value is personal independence.

6.3 The Presidents

In the final portion of the interview, Peters responds to the first opportunity to display his conservative ideology. His assessment of the presidents of the United States was particularly vehement in his criticism of Woodrow Wilson (Sound 31).

Sound 31. Available at www.cambridge.org/conversationswithstrangers

WL: So you were born in '89? You must have voted for Wi – in Wilson's election.

BP: Yes I did vote for Wilson and I was ten times – ten thousand times sorry I ever voted for him.

WL: That was 1914.

BP: 1916.

WL: 16, 16, right.

BP: Yes sir. I was ten thousand times sorry … I voted for him.

WL: Because he said he was gonna keep us out of the war?

BP: That's right. And thirty-seven days after he took the oath of office we were in a war, tryin' t' kill the best people on earth. Yes sir! . an' I don't hesitate to say that.

WL: You don't feel that the war was justified at all.
BP: I do not!!

It turned out that Peters came from a Pennsylvania German family himself, which probably explains his view of the Germans as "the best people on earth." He goes on to exhibit his rhetorical powers in his criticism of several other presidents, leading up to his condemnation of Franklin Roosevelt, and finishing with an assertion that I should "keep that thing on" so that his opinions can be heard by anyone (Sound 32).

Sound 32. Available at www.cambridge.org/conversationswithstrangers

BP: We have not had a president … for a long, long time. **WOODROW WILSON** to me was an outlaw! I don't care what you say. And **HARDING, HARDING,** I didn't like **HARDING.** But **CALVIN COOLIDGE** yes. **HERBERT HOOVER,** no! **FRANKLIN DELANER,** if that son of a bitch had been dead before he was born, it'd been better, to me. And then this **HARRY TRUMAN.** And **IKE!** I am one that didn't like **IKE!!**
WL: Well that's unusual, most people, whether they –
BP: I know, they like **IKE,** but not me. And I don' like, I didn' like **KENNEDY,** an' I didn't like, uh, **JOHNSON.** You know, you can keep that thing on as far as I'm concerned about that,'cuz I don't like, what I don't like I don't like, and you can – I don't care who knows that I don't like that outlaw.

6.4 The Bill Peters Effect

Bill Peters' use of complex syntax is not the only aspect of his language that displays unusual features. We will now turn to his sensitivity to the changes occurring in the sound system of his dialect. This has been labeled the "Bill Peters Effect" (Labov, Karan, and Miller 1991; Labov 1994: 363). Throughout the interview, Peters made a distinction between the vowels of words like "hock" and "hawk," a pattern that was typical of his generation. At that time, young people in the Duncannon area were beginning to speak differently, rhyming the two in what is called a merger of the sounds (Herold 1990), in a sound change that was expanding from Western Pennsylvania. Bill Peters displayed a remarkable reflection of the patterns of younger speakers. When I asked him to read separate words in pairs, a context that favors increased attention to speech, he appeared to have perceived the pattern of the younger generation and adopted it. We can now hear him in his reading style, saying "Don, Dawn, cot, caught" with identical vowels. On the other hand, Peters retained the distinction between the two in his spontaneous speech, as we hear in the two different vowel sounds in "sorry" and "born" in his discussion of the presidents (Sound 33).

Sound 33. Available at www.cambridge.org/conversationswithstrangers

It remains to be seen whether there is any connection between Peters' syntactic abilities and his sensitivity to the phonology of younger speakers.

When I finally packed my gear and made my way to his front porch, Bill Peters gave me a genial leave taking, but renewed his insistence that his opinions about the presidents be made public (Sound 34).

Sound 34. Available at www.cambridge.org/conversationswithstrangers

WL: Well Mr. Peters I want to thank you very much. It's been a great pleasure talking to you and I've learned ten times as much as I –
BP: Only one thing I'm sorry,
WL: What's that?
BP: that you turned that thing off when I was expressing my opinions on the presidents. I don't like it.
WL: No I didn't turn it off! I just turned it down a little bit, because you were startin' to shout a little bit and I didn' want it to, to get distorted. I didn't turn it off. Not a bit.
BP: And I don't care who you take it and repeat that to.
WL:There's not –
BP: I'm only speaking for **me** now, not her or anybody else.
WL: Of course.

Bill Peters was well aware that most of the readers of this Element would disagree with him, and that his opinions would not persuade us, nor we him. But he reached a high level of eloquence, which served him well.

7 Rural Utah: Brad Anders, Dairy Farmer

In traveling through the farmlands and forests of the United States, I learned to deal with a wide range of material matters. Now approaching the countryside dominated by Mormon (LDS) settlers, I was prepared to engage more directly with spiritual affairs. I soon learned that those settlers are well equipped to deal with a stranger who was interested in what they had to say.

Toward the end of February 1969, I was driving through the countryside of Utah, about twenty miles from Salt Lake City. I thought that it would be good to interview someone outside of the city, in a small town where the beliefs and customs of the Mormon church were held most strictly. The most characteristic features of the English spoken in that area would most likely be found in small towns.

I was cruising down a country road not far from Farmington, then a small town of less than 10,000, when I saw a grey-haired man of about sixty sitting on the porch of his farmhouse and satisfying our definition of "not doing anything in particular." I parked and approached him, and asked if he could help me find out how people did things in that part of the country — not the same as in the East where I was from. The milk cans outside the barn suggested that he was a dairy farmer, which was indeed the case. As the conversation proceeded, I learned that he was a man of many skills and trades.

7.1 The Family Farm

Brad Anders was a genial, outspoken man with a deep, resonant voice that registers elegantly to this day in the audio file digitized from the original recording. He was born in that very farmhouse, as was his father. His father's father came from New England as a convert to the LDS among the first settlers. There was no disagreement when I remarked, "So you're about as local a guy as I can find." It provoked him to make some observations on the history of the town, alerting me to the fact that I had met with someone who had a lot to say about the world around him. Anders regretted the fact that the farmland had been split up as a result of people dividing their farms among their children (Sound 35).

Sound 35. Available at www.cambridge.org/conversationswithstrangers

> One of the hard things here is the fact that eh, many of the first settlers, when they, they split their, what they started out with up with their children and their children split it up and so, then this one sells a little bit and, you can't get a farm all in one place.

When he finished high school, Anders filled a two-year LDS mission, served four years in the armed forces, in the Air Corps, and then got a degree in Aeronautics. Though he qualified as a mechanic, his first love was farming and he returned happily to the family dairy farm.

Sound 36. Available at www.cambridge.org/conversationswithstrangers

> I had no desire really to be a mechanic and yet I can do it. I like, I like it. I've overhauled tractors and things like that. It isn't I can't do it, but I, I always loved farming and ... trying t'see if I couldn't knock my head against my own, own figures and do a little better.

At the time of this interview, Anders was managing thirty-five to forty-five cows, selling up to a ton and a quarter of milk every day. He combined an experimental approach to farming with the resistance to regulation of the small businessman.

Sound 37. Available at www.cambridge.org/conversationswithstrangers

> It'll be a sad thing for the United States, as far as that goes, our country, if the time ever comes when all the farms are owned by big corporations, because then they will say to the people, "You will pay us so much, or else." And at the present time, it's sad the other way, because everything that I sell, somebody tells me how much they'll give me. Everything that I buy, somebody tells me how much I'll pay them.

7.2 A Light to Steer By

In the midst of my inquiry into his farming history, Anders turned the conversation to the theme that would dominate this interview: his investment in the Mormon church. In contrasting the LDS philosophy with that of other faiths, he emphasized its commitment to the continuous acquisition of knowledge (Sound 38).

Sound 38. Available at www.cambridge.org/conversationswithstrangers

> Around here, mostly people eh, the church has been more their, their main thing. We believe that a man is saved no faster than he gains knowledge. So that we believe that ah, the man should learn as much as he can about many things, rather than just uh, one thing. He should … try to learn more all the time, every day. We should never stop growing and progressing.

Anders' prose is suffused with the language of Mormon scripture, not only single words and phrases, but entire sentences. His discussion of the importance of the church in daily life echoes a phrase from LDS founder Joseph Smith: "a man is saved no faster than he gains knowledge."[20] In recounting his experiences on an LDS mission, he speaks of the lodgings where he lived with his missionary partner as "our place of abode"; his discussion of the New Testament Book of Revelations mentions that "it isn't time for their fulfillment yet"; he states that death and hell "delivered up the dead which were in them" and refers to "the hosts of heaven who followed Lucifer."

7.3 Spreading the Word

It was clear that the church played an important part in his daily life. I followed up with a question about whether there had been an event in his life that confirmed his conviction, and he responded with a vivid account of what

---

[20] The wording of Joseph Smith, available on several websites, differs with Anders' in only one word, where Anders says "gains knowledge" and Smith "gets knowledge." www.deseret.com/1989/8/12/20761328/prophet-teaches-that-man-is-saved-no-faster-than-he-gets-knowledge.

happened (Sound 39). It took place in a living room where he and his missionary partner were expounding the Mormon doctrine.

Sound 39. Available at www.cambridge.org/conversationswithstrangers

> While I was filling a mission for the church, in fact, something – One night someone was heckling me. You know that happens, and people, in a meeting, they were – It was just a small little meeting in a home but, a young lady who was going to college thought she was … real smart. She had asked me a question and I said I didn't know. And eh … lots of people eh, worry about the Book of Revelations more than the Mormons do. We believe in continued revelation; but as to worry about tryin' to explain all the revelations of John the Revelator. All of them … some of them haven't – it isn't time for their fulfillment yet so they haven't come. And this is the thing some of them want you to explain and – So if somebody asked me a question I didn't know, I just honestly told them I didn't know. But she kept coming back to this, and coming back to this and I'll tell you what it was so as you'll see that the answer was logical. It was reasonable. But just as sure as I'm standing here, **I did not know** [*spoken deliberately*] the answer to that until the words were put in my mouth.

In this account, we get some idea of the kind of give-and-take that occurs between the missionary and his target (Sound 40).

Sound 40. Available at www.cambridge.org/conversationswithstrangers

> And eh … it referred to the time when … John the Revelator was telling about the sea giving up the dead that which were in them. And death and hell delivered up the dead which were in them, and eh … Then there was those whose names were not found written in the Book of Life who were cast into the sea of outer darkness. And of course the question different people had asked me, and I'd always – honestly said I don't know, who they are. So she kept coming back to this. We tried to go on with what we were doing and – just leave it. But I had told her I didn't know, but she wouldn't listen. So finally I said well eh, – She brought it up again … . And before I could think, or anything else, I said to her, "Those whose names were not found written in the Book of Life were the third of the hosts of heaven who followed Lucifer … in the pre-existent world. And uh, their names were not found written in the Book of Life because they never had life here." And you know, after that – I told her that, I thought "Oh boy that – that's true!" It was just like somebody turned a great big 150 watt light globe on up here in my brain.

The force of this experience was confirmed for Anders by the reaction of his partner when they were on their home (Sound 41).

Sound 41. Available at www.cambridge.org/conversationswithstrangers

I recognized it as true and eh … We always traveled … in pairs, so my companion said to me, after we – (now this shut her up, she never said another word, that was sufficient). And when I got outside, going back to our place of abode, why my companion said to me, "Where did you read that?" I says, "What?" He said, "That answer you gave that young lady?" And I said, "I didn't read it." And uh, he said, "Well where'd you get it?" And I said, "I guess if there was ever an instance where a fella received a revelation, I did! "Because" I says "it was put right in – those … words come, were put in my mouth. I didn't even recognize … how true they were till after I said them.

This positive outcome of Anders' story rhymes with the steady commitment of the Mormon community to increasing its knowledge base.

7.4 Matters of Life and Death

Anders continued with an account of how matters of life and death were treated within the LDS perspective of his own family. He told me of a case where they were severely tested (Sound 42). His four children had contracted a blood disease. Apparently this had been a very close call.

Sound 42. Available at www.cambridge.org/conversationswithstrangers

Well they all came down with this rare type blood disease, and I had, eh, had them in the Children's Hospital all at once. And they all had to have their spleens out. And we took them in, two at a time. And, you asked about, this one, times when they disagreed, this one boy, he says – when we uh, when we took them in, my father and I we believe in administering to the sick and, as men holding the priesthood, my father and I administered to them before they – we took them in to operate on them and, they uh, he said to me the day before he was gonna be operated on, he says "What if things don't turn out all right, Dad?" And I says, "Well now look son, they're going to … I feel that they're going to … Your grandpa and I administered to you and uh, there was a blessing given to you and you're going to be all right." He says, "Yes but just supposing they don't?" And I says, "Alright, just supposing they don't. If that happens," I says, "there'll be those on the other side who'll be just as happy to see you as we'll be sad to see you go." I says, "My mother's there, your mother's mother's there, your mother's father's there, you have a brother there." I said, "There's no … no doubt but what they'll be … happy to see you again." So … eh … this satisfied him.

In Anders' speech, scriptural phrases remind us how the language of everyday life is rooted in a religious framework, and his measured rhythm contributes to the judicious air of his pronouncements. This is particularly clear in the passage where he explains to his son what might happen if he dies, each phrase ending with a rising intonation:

My mother's there,
your mother's mother's there,
your mother's father's there,
you have a brother there.

The lengthy pauses that he takes while carefully considering what he is going to say next, and the rising intonation and volume at the end of each phrase, are an invitation to any hearer to understand, and perhaps agree with, Brad Anders' point of view.

8 Hillsborough, North Carolina: Adolphus Hester, Farmer

In the spring of 1971, I was engaged in an exploration of the language of Black speakers in the hill country outside of Hillsborough, North Carolina. I picked Hillsborough because it was the site of the first dissertation on phonological variation in a Black community (Anshen 1969). In the course of traveling through the region, I found myself sitting in a country grocery store, in the company of several older Black men, discussing the eloquence of preaching. One of the men was a preacher himself. I finally put to him the question that was uppermost in my mind. "Reverend, you have heard many preachers, Black and White, in your time. Who would you say has the power of the word?" He said, "Well I couldn't say." I followed with: "But you are a *professional*. You have to say." The preacher hesitated, then said, "Well I have to admit it – we in the lead!"

In the course of the talk that followed, he suggested that I visit his uncle, Adolphus Hester.[21] I found Hester, a farmer in his early eighties, and interviewed him in his farmhouse. I learned that Hester's father died in his infancy, and his mother, left to raise him on her own, obtained work on a farm belonging to a White family. He lived there between the ages of three and nineteen, and says that he was well treated, but ended up having "mighty little" schooling. Adolphus Hester stands out in our records in his ability to negotiate between the prejudices of bureaucrats and the hard realities of Southern soil.

8.1 An Experimental Approach to Farming

In his experimental approach to farming, Hester has a lot in common with Brad Anders of Section 7, who told me he was always "tryin t'see if I couldn't knock my head against my own, own figures and do a little better." After experimenting

---

[21] Another extract from the conversation with Adolphus Hester can be found in my book *The Language of Life and Death* (Labov 2013: 102–106), which deals with his anticipation of the unexpected recovery of his mother from a long illness.

with three different ways of treating his fields, Hester says modestly, "If I try a thing, I think I'm right, I won't tell nobody it is right, I just keep looking."

By the 1930s, the "blue mold" (*Peronospora hyoscyami*)[22] had become a major problem for the humid agricultural states like North Carolina, threatening both corn and tobacco. When I asked Hester if he was still growing tobacco, he answered vigorously that he had already carried out his own experiments to control the blue mold. He had taken three tobacco fields and treated them differently: he burned the first field to the ground before replanting it; the second was left untreated; the third received no commercial fertilizer, just chicken litter and ashes.

Where Hester differs from Anders is in their exposure to formal education: as a college graduate, Anders never uses double negatives. Like Michael Duffy, with only two years of schooling, Hester uses double negatives categorically. Several examples occur in the next excerpt: *I didn't have no blue mold on it*; *I didn't use no fertilizer*; *and I didn't have no blue mold on that*; *I won't tell nobody it is right*.

Sound 43. Available at www.cambridge.org/conversationswithstrangers

WL: Well have you changed your way of growin' tobacco, now are you still doin' it?

AH: Well I'm still doin' about like I did. I ain't raisin' much, but, if I was raisin' a whole lot, I don't think I'd change it much.

WL: Well what about the blue mold, now? You uh, they have this gas treatment I gather.

AH: Why yes, they got this gas treatment. And, I reckon it's a help. But uh, I'll tell you what I did one time, I had uh, three plant beds down here. And I tooken uh, **burnt**[23] one down here, and I didn't have no blue mold on it. And I tooken, got up one, down here, there, and the blue mold just eat it up. And I decided, then I got up – one up there and I didn't use no fertilizer. I used chicken litter,[24] and ashes, and I didn't have no blue mold on that. That was the best bed of all of them. I's kinda, had it in my head, I don't know, I'm, it's I, if I try a thing, I think I'm right, I won't tell nobody it is right, I just keep lookin'. I sowed a bed out there, and I planted, well, three acres of tobacco for it, and I didn't use a bit of fertilizer.

---

[22] The Wikipedia article on blue mold details the effects of the epidemic on agriculture: "In 1960, a blue mold epidemic spread in approximately eleven countries. There was approximately twenty-five million dollars in losses which is nearly thirty percent of tobacco plants at the time" (https://en.wikipedia.org/wiki/Peronospora_hyoscyami_f.sp._tabacina).

[23] Hester's pronunciation of *burnt* here echoes the extreme pronunciation of the same vowel before *r* of Michael Duffy in the word *first*.

[24] Chicken manure.

Hester's dealing with the blue mold in a methodical and innovative experiment was not the only time he used his experience to guarantee success in farming.

8.2 The Exchange with the County Agent

In the case of the tobacco fields that were attacked by blue mold, we've seen what Hester can do in terms of concrete procedures with farming techniques. But he also has to deal with the prejudices of people who don't think much of him. He gives the illusion that he was following the directions of others when in fact he is waiting for the real world to prove him right. This is nowhere clearer than what he tells us about how a county agricultural agent who came to instruct him about the best way to plant a corn crop (Sound 44).[25] He lets us know that the agent's instructions were not necessary for someone with his experience. In the next exchange, he reports obeying the instructions to the letter, and replies with the "Yes sir" that was the standard response of an earlier period. But again, he did a parallel planting, the same method as with tobacco. Hester's story is here transcribed according the format of narrative analysis in Labov (2013), which reveals the way Hester organizes his story, clause by clause, adding details that come to be evaluated only in the final conclusion. In this first part of the story, we hear how Hester set up his parallel planting.

8.2.1 Preparing to Plant the Corn Crop

Sound 44. Available at www.cambridge.org/conversationswithstrangers

a. Now I had a county agent come out here, about 15, 16 years ago,
b. and they was goin' around, tellin' you how to raise a corn crop,
c. and uh, how to plant it, when to plant it, and when to work it.
d. And uh, they told me what kind of corn to get,
e. And I told him I didn't mind him bringing the corn.
f. And so he did,
g. he bought the corn,
h. I think the fella brought the corn from Raleigh,
i. And the fella come up here
j. and showed me how to plant it.
k. Now I'd been plantin' corn there since I was seven years old.

---

[25] The exchanges between Hester and the County Agent were a product of the New Deal, a program instituted by the Roosevelt administration to revive agriculture during the Great Depression of the 1930s. Many of our conservative country people reacted against the Soil Bank, which removed land from productivity, but others profited from technical exchange.

l. But he showed me **how** to plant it. [laughs]

m. I went ahead and planted it just like he told me,

n. and he said

o. "Now I don't want you to, I don't want you to plow that this deep,

p. Only plow it three time but not plow it this deep."

q. I told him "Yes sir."

r. And uh, I fixed the ground,

s. so they said they were satisfied at it,

t. I planted the acre.

u. And I went over twelve rows, only small rows,

v. I went over twelve rows, only small rows,

w. and planted a **me** acre, **my** way.

x. Only I didn'– they used up to 350 pound fertilizer to the acre,

y. and I didn't use but 200 pound!

z. Well I plowed mine like I wanted to plow it.

8.2.2 Results of the Experiment.

At this point, I asked him a question about how deep he planted the experimental plot, and he supplied a detailed account of what he did (Sound 45). The double shovel he mentions in this part of the narrative was a piece of farm equipment I had never heard of before, but a web search revealed that it was a horse-pulled plow, patented in 1884 and used to plow two furrows at a time, as depicted in Figure 1. It was still in use well into the twentieth century in rural North Carolina.

Sound 45. Available at www.cambridge.org/conversationswithstrangers

WL: You went about three inches deep?

AH:

aa. No suh, I took n' turn the plow

bb. and slide mine over just as close as I could get it.

cc. Then took the double shovel

dd. and put it right down there, one hoe in that furrow,

ee. and the other hoe throwed some dirt right back to that corner,

ff. and I plowed with that double shovel, just as deep as I could get it.

gg. It – come a little shower of rain,

hh. and then it set off dry,

ii. and that corn never did wither.

jj. My acre didn't.

kk. But his'n just scratchin' around there on the top,

ll. and uh, it withered.

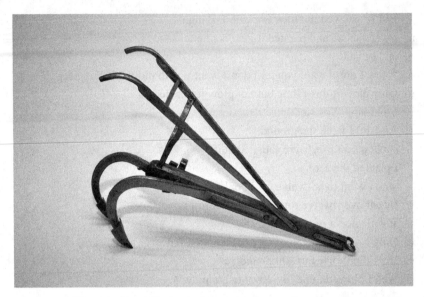

Figure 1 "Double shovel" plow of the late nineteenth and early twentieth centuries.

mm. and, then, when he come, come out here to **meas**ure the corn,

nn. he uh, said he didn't want a tad back,

oo. that I beat him so far,

pp. asked me could he get, a hundred ears out of mine out there,

qq. where I plowed like I wanted.

rr. To help the county agent

ss. and the man wan- [AH and WL both laughing] he didn't want it said that –

tt. 'course I was aiming to sell some of mine to uh, put in and have it weighed,

uu. and they knowed what it was,

vv. but uh I wouldn't have done it.

Throughout this account, Hester has many ways of telling us that one is not to take seriously the point of view of officious outsiders. Gleefully finishing this story about the county agent, he lets us know that he followed instructions to the letter, even replying "Yes sir," but that his own procedure proved him to have come out on top.

8.3 A Note on "Rural Shortening"

For Hester, the unstressed vowels of many words are frequently contracted, which makes the stream of speech somewhat difficult to follow for outsiders. In rural dialects throughout the United States, the stream of speech seems to leave a space for this "silent vowel." *The* is twice deleted in the phrase: *I think (the)*

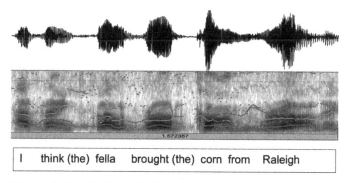

| I | think (the) fella | brought (the) corn | from | Raleigh |

Figure 2 "Rural shortening" in the speech of Adolphus Hester

fella brought (the) corn from Raleigh. We can hear that phrase again, and examine the image of the sound file (Sound 46) in Figure 2. The phrase "I think the fella brought the corn from Raleigh" lines up with the bursts of sound, and the two instances where we might have heard "the" are in fact silent. The blue line that represents the presence of audible sound is interrupted completely where these two words would have been pronounced.

Sound 46. Available at www.cambridge.org/conversationswithstrangers

In most dialects, the vowel of *the* would be quite short, but still remains as a syllable nucleus. In dialects with shortening, the syllable nucleus disappears. Other examples abound in Hester's speech. This pattern of "rural shortening" is quite general in the vernacular of many rural areas: I have observed it in the speech of a hunter in rural New Hampshire, a gas station attendant in south-western Louisiana, and a farmer in East Texas: in this volume it also occurs in the speech of Louise Atkins of Knoxville (Section 9).[26]

8.4 Hester's Rhetoric

The tone of Hester's rhetoric is understated, with an undercurrent of humor always ready to break through to the surface. I wasn't given the opportunity to object when he applied his gentle teasing to poke a little fun at me. In a discussion of how the natural world affected the rhythm of planting, he said that crops were more successful when they are planted on the waxing of the moon. He interrupted himself to ask me a rhetorical question: "You know the moon?" There was nothing for me to do but join in the laughter of everyone present.

---

[26] Hester and Atkins grew up only about 300 miles apart, and the fact that they share this feature may be of interest for further research about its history and development among both Black and White speakers of eastern Appalachia (see also Wolfram 2013).

His storytelling technique fits this pattern perfectly. Nowhere does he overtly criticize the county agent. Instead, he crafts his story to reveal that in the final test, the county agent had to admit that Hester's methods of planting and cultivating a corn crop had had a far better outcome. The result was so overwhelming that Hester had no need to have his own corn weighed and measured, graciously letting the facts speak for themselves. As he says, he wouldn't have rubbed it in.

9 Knoxville, Tennessee: Louise Atkins, Domestic Worker

In the late spring of 1977, I found myself heading into the Upper South, in search of a deeper understanding of the speech of the Southern Midlands.[27] On the outskirts of Knoxville, I met Louise Atkins, a woman in her fifties. She was hoeing her garden, but agreed to spend some time chatting with me when I stopped and introduced myself. I had not heard more than a few sentences before I realized that I had opened the door to a powerful exponent of the language and culture of Appalachia.

Born during the Depression, Atkins grew up in poverty and by the early 1950s found herself a young wife with three small children. She explained that her husband's paycheck went straight into a local bar, so she had to earn the money to pay for the basic needs of the family (Sound 47).

Sound 47. Available at www.cambridge.org/conversationswithstrangers

> I had to work! I went over and I worked a little bit, you know, in the kitchen at restaurants, and then I took in ironin', washin', babysittin'.

Under these circumstances, her children also learned the value of work (Sound 48).

> My kids had to work, they know what work is, there ain't no lie about it. They'd get out – Jimmy wanted a bicycle, he had to get a paper route, save his money and get it. In other words they was raised hard.

Sound 48. Available at www.cambridge.org/conversationswithstrangers

At the time of the interview, Atkins was divorced, living with her adult daughter and her family, enjoying her grandchildren and no longer having to provide for her own support. As she put it, she was "too old to work and too young for Social Security." Both her sons had steady jobs: one a mid-level manager in a furniture company and the other a municipal worker for the city.

---

[27] For further information on the speech patterns of the area, see Wolfram and Christian 1976; Reed 2014; Montgomery 1989, 2014. Rare audio recordings of speakers from the area made by Joseph Sargent Hall in 1939 are available on the Appalachian English website at http://artsandsciences.sc.edu/appalachianenglish/node/787.

9.1 Vietnam is Hard

You may well find Atkins' speech to be the most challenging of any of our speakers to understand. She spontaneously produces complex sentences, expressed in the vernacular of oral language transmission with little or no influence of school-based standard English. There will be more to say about this after we have listened to excerpts from her account of her youngest son's experience of volunteering for service in Vietnam. Charlie, the baby of the family, confronted her at the age of seventeen and threatened to run away unless she signed the paperwork to allow him to enlist in the army (Sound 49).

Sound 49. Available at www.cambridge.org/conversationswithstrangers

> I told Charlie, when he come home, told me he wanted me t'sign, he said "I'll run away if y'don't."

In this argument between parent and child, the phonetics of the South Midland[28] shift to an extreme form that is difficult for outsiders to comprehend. To understand more clearly, you may want to click on Sound 50 a number of times. Atkins explained to me that Charlie's threat was something she refused to accept.

Sound 50. Available at www.cambridge.org/conversationswithstrangers

> And that's som'pn my kids don't tell me. You don't tell me you wan' do som'pn. I'll do it for you. And I'll help you.

Atkins did sign the papers. Charlie was successful in volunteering to fight in Vietnam, and when he returned, he said that it had been a great experience. Atkins told me she knew other young men who had been drafted and who did not share Charlie's view. She summed up the discussion by generalizing that if somebody volunteers, they'd better like it. She expressed this as a threat, without the understood conditional "if." In summing up her evaluation of Charlie's experience, she gives me her opinion in a compact set of three clauses.

Sound 51. Available at www.cambridge.org/conversationswithstrangers

> And you volunteer to go in there, you gotta like it. 'Cos you didn't have no business to volunteer in the first place.

Much of the difficulty in understanding Louise Atkins is in the frequent deletion of unstressed vowels that are intact in other dialects. As mentioned in Section 8.3, this is a pattern she shares with Adolphus Hester. Both omit vowels in unstressed syllables and sometimes the entire syllable disappears, although

---

[28] For further details, see Wolfram and Christian 1976; Montgomery 2014; Reed 2014.

their speech styles are different in other ways. Hester's speech is slow and measured, whereas Atkins has a rapid-fire, staccato delivery. The staccato effect is achieved by reducing the short vowels and firing off the remaining syllables in a shotgun fashion. In this excerpt, Louise pronounces "*go in*" as only one syllable, where the vowel of *go* is heard as a w: *gwin*. And in the sentence following, the vowel of *to* in"*to volunteer*" is deleted. This sentence is held together by words that you don't hear.

9.2 The Problem with Young Preachers

Uppermost in Atkins' view of community life was the church. She was raised a Baptist, but her family members attended a variety of churches, and she didn't approve of the hard line taken by the young preachers in her son's church (Sound 52).

Sound 52. Available at www.cambridge.org/conversationswithstrangers

LA: So these new modern churches, I don't understand the preachers.
WL: Really!
LA: I can't understand them.
WL: How come?
LA: They just don't preach like the ones I wanna go. Now when Mother went, there was one right over here and they called it the Hard Shell Baptists. I mean they didn't have no music. The preacher he preached, and the singers they sung, and that shoutin' was for real, 'cause it was no music in that church, I mean no pianos, no nothin', and they called theirselves the Hard Shell Baptists. And I mean when that song was sung, and the people got up for shoutin', that was from the heart.

Her major objection to "these young preachers" was that they claim to know who is going to hell, and she was particularly incensed at their claims that celebrities like Elvis Presley would be going to hell (Sound 53).

Sound 53. Available at www.cambridge.org/conversationswithstrangers

Or I don't like these, that talks, and, and puts people, what, tells people people's goin' to hell. When they don't know whether they are or not. I don't know or you don't know whether people's goin' to hell or not.

Atkins insisted that it's impossible to know who is going to hell, because you can be saved "in the twinkle of an eye." She told me she had learned this from her mother, who had read "from one end of that Bible to the other."

9.3 School Integration in Knoxville

Atkins told me that the local schools were segregated when her children were in school, but that by now, the school her four grandchildren attended was integrated. She took a positive view of integration.

Sound 54. Available at www.cambridge.org/conversationswithstrangers

> I'd rather have a Colored teacher teaching my grandkids than White ones, they're meaner to them. I can't stand a White teacher over my kids, over these grandkids of mine.

She continued on this theme by making an explicit comparison between Black and White teachers, saying "the Colored teachers are a heck of a lot better to the White kids ... than the White teachers are."

9.4 Wrestling

Atkins was a prominent figure at the weekly wrestling matches she attended with her son Jimmy and his family every Friday night (Sound 55).

Sound 55. Available at www.cambridge.org/conversationswithstrangers

LA: Yep! I tell y' what, don't never get behind me if you ever come to wrestlin' around here.
WL: Oh really?
LA: Specially when I got – when two of my guys are in there, I'm crazy about, and somebody else is in there. 'Cause, they tell **me** I get kinda **wild** out there.

I suggested that there are people who get put off "because they say it's all show business" (Sound 56).

Sound 56. Available at www.cambridge.org/conversationswithstrangers

> Well, some of it is, now really, I have seen a lot of it out there that's fake, but there's a lot of it that's not fake.

I asked her if she ever lost her voice hollerin' at the wrestling matches (Sound 57).

Sound 57. Available at www.cambridge.org/conversationswithstrangers

WL: I bet you lose your voice, hollerin', huh?
LA: Yep! Ever' Friday night. Takes me – let's see – today's Tuesday, I'm just now gettin' my voice back. And I get – they say I get real **weird** out there.

Even her own children can't control her (Sound 58).

Sound 58. Available at www.cambridge.org/conversationswithstrangers

> In fact I've hollered at a few of the wrestlers and they've come back at me,
> and Charles gets behind me and he says "OK mama you asked for that!"

Louise Atkins is introduced into this volume as a speaker of the dialect that has traditionally been considered the most remote from standard English: the dialect of the Southern Mountain area known variously as "Hillbilly" English, Appalachian English, or Smoky Mountain English, as documented by Hazen (2020) and on the Appalachian English website (http://artsandsciences.sc.edu/appalachianenglish). It is identified in the *Atlas of North American English* (Labov, Ash, and Boberg 2006) as South Midland English. It is differentiated from Southern English by the consistent pronunciation of *r* as a consonant (in contrast to the New Yorkers we heard from in Sections 3 and 4, and Southerners like Henry Guyton of Section 10). Louise Atkins may be recognized as a speaker of South Midland English immediately by her consistent use of its sound pattern, and particularly by the "vowel shortening" pattern discussed earlier.

Atkins' spontaneous use of language reveals her as someone who commands a wide range of linguistic resources. In her negative sentences, though she occasionally has a standard sentence like:

> Now they don't care **anything** about wrestling.

she generally uses double negatives, like

> I **can't** say **nothin'** bad against him.

And the transcript of her interviews contains several instances of negative inversion:

> **Ain't nobody** gonna live a perfect life.

In past tense negatives, *ain't* is her normal auxiliary:

> The man **ain't been** in there too long.

In standard English, statements of existence begin with what is sometimes called a "dummy" *there,* and Atkins usually uses that pattern:

> But there's a lot of it that's not fake.
> He said, "There's one fat one and a whole bunch of skinny ones."

However, in such "existential" statements, her usage is variable, and is sometimes expressed with a dummy *it*:

> It was no music in that church.

This section has projected many ways of looking at the language of Louise Atkins: as a church member, a parent and grandparent, a community member, and a wrestling fan. It was evident from the start that she is voluble: she uses her command of English to control children, parents, teachers, and neighbors. They all treated her as a formidable force. Atkins was proud of her Southern Mountain heritage. She used its resources to paint us a picture of her triumph over the obstacles of her life.

10 East Atlanta, Georgia: Henry Guyton, Railway Foreman

In the fall of 1970 I was traveling through the Lower South with the idea that I might be able to interview speakers with strongly developed patterns of the local dialect of the area. I had heard that urban Atlanta had been heavily influenced by immigration from the north, so I drove through the suburban town of East Atlanta, away from the city center. There I found Henry Guyton tending to his garden, a stout, gray-haired man in working clothes. I introduced myself as someone interested in the changes that were taking place in the New South; he introduced me to his son Henry, who didn't say much, and to his wife.

Guyton was born in 1912 into a family of railroad workers. At thirteen, he was working for a dollar and a half a day[29] as a water boy for his grandfather, who was section foreman. He attended a country school, where two or three grades were often taught in the same room. He graduated high school when he was sixteen, and then went to work as a mechanic for the Southern Railroad, a job he felt he was born to do. Guyton stayed with the Southern Railroad for forty-three years. At the time of the interview, at fifty-eight years old, he was working as a foreman in the railroad yards. Guyton did not believe that anything he had learned in school had been useful to him in his job with the railroad, and was strong in his conviction that mechanics are born, not made (Sound 59). He told me how he already had all the skills he needed at the age of thirteen.

10.1 Mechanics Are Born, Not Made

Sound 59. Available at www.cambridge.org/conversationswithstrangers

> When I was 13 years old, they had bought a T-model Ford. Well I tore it down one week, and I went down to my aunt's, and stayed down there, durin' the summer, I'd say 6 or 8 weeks. And it was piled up in the, in the garage, a little shed there. Well I come back home, I put that car back together and it run, and I'd been away from it 6 weeks, and I wadn't but 13 years old. And it run! That's the reason I say it, a man is born a mechanic, he's not – he don't study it, it just come natural to him.

I asked him whether that was still the case (Sound 60).

Sound 60. Available at www.cambridge.org/conversationswithstrangers

---

[29] Readers familiar with Mark Knopfler's Notting Hillbillies *Railroad Work Song* (www.youtube.com/watch?v=Pbmay3wONZc) will already have heard about "workin' on the railroad for a dollar a day."

WL: If there was a young fella that wanted to start as a mechanic today, how far do you think he should go in school?

HG:He should finish high school. That's all he needs, if he's gon' be a mechanic, is high school education. If, if he's a mechanic – now, if he's not, mechanic, – I'd say a mechanic's born! They are not picked up. You don't learn to be a mechanic, it's borned in you! To be a mechanic. Now I got one right there [pointing to son Henry] with cerebral palsy. He's a mechanic, he's a born mechanic. If he was all right, if he was a normal child, could use his hands, he'd be a mechanic, he wouldn't even have to go to school to be a mechanic. 'Cause he could just go right out there and go to work with it. Because he can do it now, as much as he can use his hands. He can go out there and tear an automobile down!

WL: No kiddin', he can do that?

HG: Yeah!

Son Henry: Mm hmm!

10.2 Premonitions

Along with Guyton's conviction that mechanics were born, not made, he held a strong belief in the value of premonitions. Like many who do, he was aware that many others do not. In the course of the evening, I asked him: "Did it ever happen, that someone had a feeling that something was going to happen, and it did happen?" He answered positively and emphatically, thumping on his chest: "I'm the one!" But before telling me of the most important event of his life, he delivered two accounts of how he had foreseen coming events (Sounds 61 and 62).

Sound 61. Available at www.cambridge.org/conversationswithstrangers

> The first one I remember I'll tell you. I was walkin' up the railroad, Dad worked up here, and we lived a mile, a half a mile from the railroad. One night, I was walkin' up the track, I met a MadDog. I'm dreamin' it now! Well for some reason or other that MadDog dodged me, and went on. And I went on off it, told Dad about it. Three weeks later I met a MadDog at the same place that I dreamed of that day, I went and he turned, just like that dog did and went over to bitin' her daddy's automobile tires when he was makin' the curve and we killed him and he was mad. I was in a hundred foot of the same place that I done that.

He then told me of a second dream that foretold the future.

Sound 62. Available at www.cambridge.org/conversationswithstrangers

And another one, I was layin' in the bed one night, and I woke up and I says uh, to my wife, I said, "Dad's had a wreck." "Oh you're crazy." He went to work at eleven o'clock. I woke up and I turned, turned to the clock, it was five minutes after eleven, I said "Dad's had a wreck." I said I dreamed he had a wreck. I got up, put on my clothes and went down and he'd run in the ditch between me and the block over to where he worked, he worked at Ellingwood. Didn't hurt him, but he was in the ditch.

10.3 I Lost My Oldest Boy

However, these were only tests of my ability to believe what he was about to tell me: a dream that came to him after the death of his son Neil (Sound 63).

Sound 63. Available at www.cambridge.org/conversationswithstrangers

> I lost my oldest boy. He was twenty years old. Died with cancer, tumor o' the brain.

He then pointed to a picture on the wall of his two sons: Neil, the son who died, and Little Henry, the one who had cerebral palsy (Sound 64).

Sound 64. Available at www.cambridge.org/conversationswithstrangers

> See his picture – that's him. That's Little Henry, that's him and that's him right there.

Guyton took a deep breath. Apparently I was ready to hear the story (Sound 65).

Sound 65. Available at www.cambridge.org/conversationswithstrangers

> So when he died with the cancer, I got sick … I thought I was gon' die myself, with a cancer. Went on there for 'bout six or eight months, an' I went to ever' doctor, they say, "Ain't nothin' wrong with you." So I went to bed one night. He come to me in a dream. He come home. We was talkin', 'n' certainly, I jus' turned around to him. I said, "Neil when you gon' come 'n' get me?" Just like that. He said, "Daddy, it's gonna be a long time before I come 'n' get you." And then I got well. An' I'm not bothered anymore about anything, don't worry about anything 'cause that day when he tell me he gon' come get me I'll know I'm ready t'go. Now if you don't b'lieve that you c'n ask my wife 'bout that. I thought I was gon' die, and everybody else did too. An' that's the only thing that do it, when he come says, "I ain't gon come n' get you for a long time Daddy." And then I got well. **And I actually believe** he'll let me know when he gets ready to come n' get me too. I got that much faith in that dream.

Guyton indicates the extent to which he expects disbelief with "Now if you don't b'lieve that." But the most remarkable demonstration of his linguistic commitment is seen in the complex structure of the clauses in this narrative that tell us when he will be ready to die, as indicated by the square brackets: "that day [when he tell me [[he gon' come get me]]], I'll know I'm ready to go." I analyze this narrative in full detail in *The Language of Life and Death* (Labov 2013).

Guyton's confidence in this dream is supported by the adverb *actually*, which reinforces assertions that are hard to otherwise accept: here, that his beloved son will appear to him as the angel of death. Guyton indicated in many ways that he did not know how far I could be moved toward the state of belief that I recognized in him. There was no doubt that his powerful use of the English language gained my profound respect for his life experience.

11 Philadelphia, Pennsylvania: Celeste Sullivan, Saleswoman

In 1975–76, the study of a working-class South Philadelphia neighborhood was carried out by Anne Bower as part of the NSF-funded Language Change and Variation (LCV) project, which I reported on elsewhere (Labov 2001)[30] Early in her study of the neighborhood, Anne was introduced to Celeste Sullivan by Mae D'Alphonso, who was the secretary of the local parish and Sullivan's best friend. Anne began attending the weekly coffee klatch held at Sullivan's house, and through her, was introduced to many members of the principal social networks on the Clark Street block (Labov 2001: 386).

In a sociometric analysis based on participants' naming of friendships, Sullivan was at the center of social networks on Clark Street (Labov 2001: 350). She was also a leader in the sound changes going on in Philadelphia. In our original study of Sullivan's speech, we used measurements of *can't*, *canteen*, *serviceman*, *stand*, *dance*, *mad*, and *bad* to show how Sullivan advanced the vowel change in progress with these words (Labov 2001; Labov, Rosenfelder, and Fruehwald 2013). The acoustic measurements of her vowels showed her to be the leader of the other eight women in her communication network.

11.1 Dealing with the Adult World

Sullivan's many accounts reflect the rigid norms of her Italian-American family. Her father, a shoemaker, had rules that governed his wife and herself, his only child (Sound 66).

Sound 66. Available at www.cambridge.org/conversationswithstrangers

CS: Well, you weren't allowed to talk while you were eating. As soon as he walked in the door the food had to be on the table, and it had to be hot.

---

[30] Bower's (1984) dissertation drew on this fieldwork.

My mother had to be there. My mother could never be out. Never. There would be murder. And we sat down, and we ate. And you couldn't laugh, and you couldn't talk, until dinner was over.

AB: Then what did you do after dinner?

CS: Go into the parlor and listen to the radio. To the news.

AB: He left you and your mom in here, right?

CS: No, we had to sit in the parlor and listen to the news with him.

AB: When did you all clean up the kitchen?

CS: Well, uh, my mother seemed – my mother never sat down to eat, Anne, 'cause she was always serving.

Here we have a paradox. By the age of fourteen, the child who was not allowed to express her opinions at the dinner table had had to leave school and go to work. Hers was a powerful voice in public disputes: a fluent exponent of the vernacular.[31] She was quick to assert her sense of right and wrong, and to defend herself when treated unfairly (Sound 67).

Sound 67. Available at www.cambridge.org/conversationswithstrangers

CS: Ah, I started out a salesgirl and got demoted to the stock room. [laughs] Well at fourteen, It was during the war. And, uh, they needed all the help they can get. And the old salesladies there, you know, they had a sale I'll never forget one day. And I made $116 and they took it away from me and gave it to this old saleslady. 'Cause I was called the contingent in the store. And I was so mad and I hollered and screamed and yelled, and they demoted me to the stock room.

AB: They took your hard-earned money!

Anne was a gifted and responsive interviewer, and as the conversation continued, Anne's responses encouraged Sullivan to talk about how she dealt with the adult world as a teenager growing up, and coming of age during World War II (Sound 68). The third speaker in this segment, "MD," is Mae D'Alphonso, Sullivan's friend.

Sound 68. Available at www.cambridge.org/conversationswithstrangers

CS: Oh that's one thing you couldn't do, is get in a car with a guy.

MD. God help you if anybody saw you!

CS: Oh you'd get killed, you'd get killed.

AB: … tattletale on you. That's crazy!

CS: Yeah because see Italian people have family all over the country.

AB: I know!

---

[31] Readers interested in Sullivan's role in sound change may want to replay her speech several times to hear the emphatic "raising" of the vowel in the word *mad* and *dance* from "short a" to "long e." I documented her leading position in short-a raising (Labov 2001: 345–49).

CS: You can't do anything. My mother used to send – I used to go to the movies and she used to send a couple of the boys up the street to watch who I used to be in the movies with.

AB: Did she really?

CS: Oh yeah.

AB: Hah hah!

CS: But we were in cahoots the boys and I.

AB: believe it!

CS: Yeah. That's the only way you could get out. Or like we'd date. I would date. And like uh my father would say [sternly]: "Where you going?" "Now daddy now look. Georgie is gonna take me," Georgie down the street, see and Daddy thought, "oh boy she's safe with Georgie." So Georgie would go his way and I would go my way.

MD: She didn't have brothers.

CS: And then we would meet, see at a certain time I said, "Georgie please, please Georgie, don't do that to me. You better be there." He'd say, "Don't worry," cuz his father was just as bad as my father – we would meet. And we'd come home like two nice little kids. But I used to go dance at the canteen.

AB:The canteen?

CS: Yeah they had a canteen that was all servicemen. And you couldn't get in if you didn't have a date. And you'd have to be a serviceman. To take you in. But once you got in you could leave this guy, you know, and dance with everybody else. And that's what we used to do: stand on in the corner. And wait for the fellas and they'd – I'd say to one of the sailors, "Are you going in there?" And he'd say, "Yeah." "Would you take me in?" "Sure!" And they would take – and nothing bad would happen in there. And the Salvation Army ran a beautiful thing. It was only coffee and donuts, there was no drinking, and soda. And music. All night you'd dance, dance, dance.

11.2 Italian Americans in World War II

World War II had a great impact on Sullivan's family. Since Italy was an enemy country, Italian Americans found themselves in a difficult position. Anne asked Sullivan where her cousins fought (Sound 69).

Sound 69. Available at www.cambridge.org/conversationswithstrangers

Ohh! That was another problem. They wouldn't send them to Italy, naturally, because they were Italian. So mostly all the boys that were Italian Americans, they'd send them out to the Pacific.

Sullivan's father had been brought to the United States as a two-month old baby. He and his siblings had never spoken Italian, and regarded themselves as loyal Americans. But the powers-that-be made it difficult for them:

Sound 70. Available at www.cambridge.org/conversationswithstrangers

> See my father never knew he wasn't a citizen of this country. No, my father thought he was born in this country. And, during the Second World War, then they found out. How they ever found out was – because my father didn't even know it. And, hhmm, they sent the FBI men over to tell him that he wasn't born in the United States, he was born in Sicily. 'Cause my grandmother had 13 children, and she didn't – she was illiterate, she didn't know, who was born in this country and who wasn't. So she said to my father, "No, you were born here." And there it was his younger brother. And there she carried my father in her arms aboard the ship to come to America. But you would never know my father was ever born in that country.

Her father's situation was dire: he was threatened with deportation (Sound 71).

Sound 71. Available at www.cambridge.org/conversationswithstrangers

CS: And when they said they wanted to deport him, for not declaring he was an enemy alien, he said, "Enemy alien! Are you kiddin'?" He said, "You gotta be kiddin! I'm no enemy alien!" And they, they had a court case and all, and my mother hadda go, and she – Oh they were in tears, my father was the best American that God ever put on this earth, I'll tell ya that boy! He was the chief of the air raid wardens and all, then he couldn't be that or anything, they took everything away from him.
AB: Oh, bless his heart!
CS: And that was a sin.

In Sullivan's account of growing up in Philadelphia, we see the intersection of her Italian ethnicity with World War II. For her parents' generation, it meant an unexpected and unwelcome breach with their attachment to American identity. We see no such effect on Sullivan: she makes her way into the canteen and in fact spots a sailor across the room that she decides to marry. She does in fact marry him: Jim Sullivan.

In her telling of how she met her husband at the servicemen's canteen during World War II, Sullivan throws all the energy of the current Philadelphia dialect, with rising vowels, expanding diphthongs, and repeated modifiers. The intonation and volume of her speech carries the authority she assumes in making people do what she wants. She organizes Georgie to cover for her when she wants to go out; she gets sailors who don't know her to take her into the canteen. In this study, we have brought the listener into touch with the emotional and social factors that drive sound change.

12 Philadelphia, Pennsylvania: Gloria Stein, Postal Clerk

When I moved to the University of Pennsylvania in 1971, I began to teach Linguistics 560, "The Study of the Speech Community," and continued almost every year until 2015. Here groups of students entered the community, made their own contacts, and conducted the interviews, according to procedures I describe elsewhere (Labov 1984). In the fall of 1981, a group of six studied a neighborhood in North Philadelphia known as Frankford. Among them were the students Chérie Francis and Paul Dietz. They interviewed Gloria Stein, the sixty-six-year-old Black woman who is the subject of this section. Listening to the recording, one is struck by the clarity of her voice and her control of the situation. Chérie, herself a Black woman, carries most of the conversation, but Paul also contributes at many points, and Gloria Stein seems very much at ease with them. A quotation from their Interview Report indicates that it was indeed a successful conversation:

> Initially she claimed she had no time, and was, grudgingly, willing to let us talk for half an hour. The interview wound up taking 90 minutes with Mrs. Stein continuing to talk with us when she walked out onto the porch.

12.1 Her Mother's Triumph

Gloria Stein's interview included an account of the terrifying events on the day her family moved into a White neighborhood in South Philadelphia. She was only ten years old, left alone to look after her younger sister and brothers (Sound 72).[32]

Sound 72. Available at www.cambridge.org/conversationswithstrangers

> Well no sooner did my mother get out of the house – my father went first – than, oh what such a – awful crash came through the window. And I, and I looked and there was a big stone. And then of course they, they … well they stoned the house. And I had sense enough to get the kids into the stairway, so that they wouldn't get hurt by flying gra– glass, and I said to them, "Now you stay there, don't move, because nothing will reach you here, and I'm gonna go and see if I can find Mom." We called our mother Mom.

After recalling these shocking events in such detail, Stein's voice grew stronger as she spoke about her mother's reactions to this news, dealing first with a policeman who happened by (Sound 73).

---

[32] This long story has been slightly edited to remove side comments, mainly about particular locations mentioned, but the account of the events has been preserved verbatim.

Sound 73. Available at www.cambridge.org/conversationswithstrangers

> And I finally found my mother. I did find her. And while I was trying to tell her what had happened, a policeman went by! And my voice was such that you could hardly make out what I was saying, I was so nervous and, and my voice was shaking so. And he wanted to find out what I, what was wrong with me. And then when he understood what the situation was, he turned to my mother and says, "It's a bad neighborhood. It's Irish," and he said, "They're known to do things like that. Better move out of there." My mother said, "I just moved in, how am I gonna move out?" He says, "I don't know," he says, "but they don't want any Black people in there." And he didn't say Black because they didn't use Black then.

A woman of great courage and resolve, Stein's mother would not take "no" for an answer (Sound 74).

Sound 74. Available at www.cambridge.org/conversationswithstrangers

> She said well, "You're the law, you're supposed to uh, protect us." And he says, "I can't do anything with it." He was Irish himself. "I can't do anything about it." So my mother said, "Where is the precinct you work from?" And he told her. So uh, she said, "Well if you can't do anything to help me, I'll go see who – if I can't find someone else to help me." Well, in those days Black people were so – cowed by circumstances and uniforms and – and – and White people, you know, they uh, many times didn't assert themselves. But thankfully my mother was not one of those kind.

When they arrived at the precinct, Stein's mother confronted the captain (Sound 75).

Sound 75. Available at www.cambridge.org/conversationswithstrangers

> My mother said, to the Captain, "What are you going to do about it?" And he says, "Well lady, there's nothing we **can** do about it." And she says, "You mean to tell me that I have to live under those circumstances, and there's nothing that you can do about it?" Uh, he said to me, "Did you see anyone?" And I said, "No." He says, "Well how can, how can you do anything, if you don't know who, who to put the blame on?" So, my mother said, "Well, I don't know what I'm going to do." She says, "But one thing I know I'm not gonna do is move, because I have no money to move with. It took all we had to, to pay the rent," and she said, "If they didn't want me there they should not have rented the house to me. Now the real estate agent should be accountable." So, anyhow, she said to him, "Well I know one thing you can do." And he said, "What's that?" She says, "You can take me home." He said, "Take you home?" She said, "Yes in the police patrol." So I guess they figured, let's get this lady out of here, because she's talking loud and long and they had never come up with anybody like that.

Figure 3 Early police patrol wagon in Philadelphia.

Like the one depicted in Figure 3, police patrol wagons at the time were drawn by a team of horses and had a clanging bell. Acting on Stein's mother's request, the police took her and little Gloria home in a great commotion. It drew a crowd: exactly what she had in mind (Sound 76).

Sound 76. Available at www.cambridge.org/conversationswithstrangers

> So, they put us in the police patrol and they took us home. And uh, of course with the horses, and the police patrol, and the clang, they had a bell that clanged, clang clang clang, you know they talk about the trolley, that went clang. Well this police patrol, that bell they had, it went, "Clang clang clang." And uh, all the neighbors came running out, to see what was happening.

Stein's story paints an unforgettable picture: her twenty-seven-year old mother on a cold winter night, facing down a crowd of hostile White people.

Sound 77. Available at www.cambridge.org/conversationswithstrangers

> And when we got out of that police patrol, before the patrol ever left my mother turned and faced ALL those people that were standing around. And she says, "Why you're doing this to me I don't know." She says, "I know that

I am different from you, color wise, but in every other respect I am just the same as you are. And all I'm trying to do is provide a home for my family." She told them that they had rented the house, she told them how much money she had paid, she had told them that was all the money she had, and they had paid that rent for a month. She knew she was going to be there for the month. She did not know beyond the month. She says, "It is winter time and it is cold. And I cannot afford to be buying windows." Now she said, "Whoever threw the stones, I don't know. But you can all see what has happened. And now I'm telling you that we're going to be here for a month. So you might just as well make up your mind to that. **If you don't want me here**, then you people get together, and give me enough money to move somewhere else. Because I do not have it." Of course you know they didn't do that. They probably didn't have any money either.

In this retelling of her mother's confrontation with the neighbors, Gloria speaks as her mother, remembering what she heard her mother say fifty-six years ago. She concludes the account of the house being stoned with evidence that the effect of her mother's speech on the neighbors must have been substantial (Sound 78).

Sound 78. Available at www.cambridge.org/conversationswithstrangers

> During the period of time that we were there, my father became sick, and the neighbors were as nice as anybody could ever have been.

12.2 Strength in Adversity

From the time she was a teenager, Gloria Stein had to deal with sexual harassment as well as racism. As a high school student, she did all kinds of part time domestic work (Sound 79).

Sound 79. Available at www.cambridge.org/conversationswithstrangers

GS: The only trouble I had was with, with many of the men in the family, chasing me all over the place. And that seemed –
CF: Oh, men in your family you –
GS: No! Where I would be working! And it seemed – one woman I went to, her husband was a tailor, he had a tailor shop and I said, "Mrs. Brooks, your husband is after me all the time!" And I said, "I'm gonna have to leave! Because I can't stand it." And she says, "Oh you know how men are, she said "don't pay any attention to him!" And she, I mean, she just took it as a matter of course!
CF: Mmhmm. You were how old then? When this happened?
GS: Well I, then was about 16. Maybe 15, somewhere in there. I was a teenager.

CF:I gather you didn't work for that family much longer?

GS: Well, I uh – no! Because I couldn't stand her husband and he was so obvious, and then after I tol – I thought, you know, telling her that would protect me, but it didn't do a thing for me. I really think she was afraid of her husband because she … she didn't sympathize with me at all, she just said, "You know how men are," but I didn't know how men were.

After graduating from Simon Gratz High School, at the height of the Depression, she got a job in a pharmacy (Sound 80).

Sound 80. Available at www.cambridge.org/conversationswithstrangers

> And you, remember the times now. There wasn't much too – much choice you had, you either – almost everything that the Black people did was menial anyhow. And you either worked or you didn't work. And I was kind of proud of working in a drugstore, because they had me doing everything in there. I learned a lot, I know I wasn't supposed to dispense uh, uh, medicine, but they had me counting and bottling. Which I, which probably was against the law, but it was a Jewish concern, and then they, they had a fountain in the store and I used to wait on the people. And uh, I didn't get paid anything extra for doing it. And it was, it was cheaper than they would have had to pay somebody else. And then if, if anybody came into the store, because Black people at that time couldn't even sit at the fountain. They would just say, "Oh that's my girl." See, so that excused me, and then the people didn't mind me being there because I was "their girl."

12.3 A Woman of Conviction

As an adult, Gloria Stein and her husband, a veteran of World War II, raised her sister's three children when they would otherwise have been put up for adoption. In. Sound 81, she admonishes the children.

Sound 81. Available at www.cambridge.org/conversationswithstrangers

> The Bible says, honor your father and your mother. Doesn't say what kind of a father or what kind of a mother. It says, honor your father and your mother. Because it'll be a blessing to you. Not because of them but because of what it'll do for you.

Stein was active in her church, and had a number of different jobs: after her husband died, she worked as a postal clerk because she "had to do something!" She also maintained her interest in language. In high school, she had studied German for four years and Latin for two. After high school, she took night classes in Spanish. When I listened to her interview, I was startled by her reflections on language (Sound 82).

Sound 82. Available at www.cambridge.org/conversationswithstrangers

> It's amazing! That as you live, as time goes by, there are idioms and things that creep into the language that weren't there before, and uh, you know, every once-in-a-while you're hearing something and you, you don't know what it is. You don't know what it is.

Gloria Stein is one of only four high-school graduates among the speakers we have dealt with here, the others being Donald Poole, Brad Anders, and Henry Guyton. Like them, she is at home in standard English, and controls its complex structures. She consistently uses the standard English markers associated with the upper middle class. Alone among the eight people the students interviewed in her neighborhood, she uses no double negatives, the others ranging between 25 and 60 percent. The students also established that her use of the informal *-in* form of the suffix *-ing* was only 3 percent (N=144), as compared with rates between 37 and 100 percent among her neighbors.

We may also recognize in her speech the power of not using contractions – a device she uses sparingly. Although there are many instances of contraction in her speech (*shouldn't*, *don't*, etc.), quoting her mother's powerful speech to the neighbors, we hear: "it is cold"; "cannot afford"; and the final "I do not have it." In the same story, she might have said: "My mother got out of the house, and right after that, an awful crash came through the window." Instead, Gloria Stein uses a subordinate clause with inversion and *do*-support: not "As soon as she got out of the house," but "No sooner did she get out of the house."

Like her mother, Gloria Stein lived in a number of different parts of Philadelphia, and seems to have had a talent for making friends with her neighbors. The following excerpt again illustrates her standard English elegance. Instead of saying "if anything happened to me," she uses the subjunctive: "if anything were to happen to me." Instead of "If I became ill," she says "should I become ill" once again inverting subject "I" and auxiliary "should." Despite the fact that such features are usually associated with formality, they never sound formal in her speech: she maintains a level of discourse that is at once intimate, spontaneous, and gracious.

Sound 83. Available at www.cambridge.org/conversationswithstrangers

> All of them I'm friendly with, that's what, why I say I wouldn't change my neighborhood. Because I know if anything ***were to happen to me***, I know that my neighbors would, would see about me, and they do, ***should I become ill or something***. And there's always somebody to bring me a bowl of soup or, or go to the store for you and I have neighbors up the street who take me every week to market. Won't take a penny for taking me.

Gloria Stein represents the aspirations of the rising middle class. She makes it clear that, being Black, she has had to work harder to make her the way in the world. Of the ten speakers we have encountered, she is the only one to have explicitly expressed her philosophy of living. It is worth listening to in its entirety (Sound 84).

Sound 84. Available at www.cambridge.org/conversationswithstrangers

> We can only do what we aspire to do. If you don't think you can, you won't, no matter what it is, if you don't think you can, you won't. And most times, if you just try, no matter what it is, try it. I mean this business of saying, "Oh I can't do and what's the use? And the world's coming to an end." I believe it is coming to an end. But I don't think you're supposed to stand still and wait for it to come to an end! You keep on going until life stops in one form or another, because we all know we're going to die, one day. But just because you're old, or just because you're sick, or just because you're handicapped, you're supposed to not keep trying and keep doing? And I think the more you do, the more you're able to do! I really do.

In selecting the speakers for this volume, many approaches to eloquence have been considered. In response to answering the question, "Why these?," Gloria Stein speaks for herself.

13 Final Words

In 1305, Dante wrote *De Vulgari Eloquentia* ("On the eloquence of the Vernacular"), the first written defense of a spoken language as worthy to be written. To prove it, he went on to write *The Divine Comedy* in that language. The ten speakers featured in the sections of this Element are also eloquent in the vernacular: they have been chosen because they had a great deal to say and had their own way of saying it. They are people who stood out in my memory as individuals. Their recorded speech was not pre-formulated, written out in advance, or the product of literary effort. The excerpts from their speech you have heard here display their spontaneous, real-time use of the vernacular – the language of their everyday life. As they talk, we hear the resources of the language being ransacked and put to use for their particular rhetorical effectiveness.

If these ten speakers had been asked to translate their experience into writing, it would have been hard – as all writing is hard. But we recognize that the spoken language can carry the agony of experience that defines the full dimension of humanity. As we listen and re-listen to the ten speakers, it becomes increasingly evident that their target is not the stranger who has appeared at their door. Someone they tolerate but who shows their ignorance of the basic facts of life at every turn of the conversation. They are addressing their peers, the people they had to do better than in the many twists and turns of the life they had lived, whether it is planting corn or outrunning a fire, confronting a crowd or outwitting an opponent in the ring. They are heard as they dealt with the people they have been measured against, and learned from. In all these circumstances, what we take away is the experience of many generations, preserved for us in the excellence, or shall we say the elegance of their language.

References

Anshen, Frank. 1969. Speech variation among Negroes in a small Southern community. PhD dissertation, New York University.

Becker, Kara. 2009. /r/ and the construction of a place identity on New York City's Lower East Side. *Journal of Sociolinguistics* 13: 634–58.

Becker, Kara. 2010. Regional dialect features on the Lower East Side of New York City: Sociophonetics, ethnicity, and identity. PhD dissertation, New York University.

Bower, Anne. 1984. The construction of stance in conflict narrative. PhD dissertation, University of Pennsylvania.

Cloward, Richard A., and Lloyd E. Ohlin. 1960. *Delinquency and Opportunity: A Theory of Delinquent Gangs*. Glencoe, IL: The Free Press.

Eckert, Penelope. 1989. *Jocks and Burnouts*. New York: Teachers College Press.

Eckert, Penelope. 2000. *Linguistic Variation as Social Practice*. Oxford: Blackwell.

Eckert, Penelope. 2018. *Meaning and Linguistic Variation*. Cambridge: Cambridge University Press.

Feagin, Crawford. 1979. *Variation and Change in Alabama English*. Washington, DC: Georgetown University Press.

Fishman, Joshua. 1966. *Language Loyalty in the U.S.* The Hague: Mouton.

Fowler, Joy. 1986. The social stratification of (r) in New York City department stores, 24 years after Labov. NYU term paper.

Goffman, Erving. 1983. Felicity's condition. *American Journal of Sociology* 89: 1–53.

Gregersen, Frans, and Inge Lise Pedersen (eds.). 1991. *The Copenhagen Study in Urban Sociolinguistics: Parts I and II*. Copenhagen: C. A. Reitzels Forlag.

Hazen, Kirk (ed.). 2020. *Appalachian Englishes in the Twenty First Century*. Morgantown: West Virginia University Press.

Herold, Ruth. 1990. Mechanisms of merger: The implementation and distribution of the low back merger in Eastern Pennsylvania. PhD dissertation, University of Pennsylvania.

Kurath, Hans, and Raven McDavid. 1963. *The Pronunciation of English in the Atlantic States*. Studies in American English 3. University of Michigan Press.

Labov, William. 1963. The social motivation of a sound change. *Word* 19: 273–309.

Labov, William. 1966. *The Social Stratification of English in New York City*. Washington, DC: Center for Applied Linguistics. Second edition published by Cambridge University Press, 2006.

Labov, William. 1984. Field methods of the project on linguistic change and variation. In John Baugh and Joel Sherzer (eds.), *Language in Use.* Englewood Cliffs: Prentice Hall, 28–53.

Labov, William. 1994. *Principles of Linguistic Change*, vol. 1, *Internal Factors.* Oxford: Basil Blackwell.

Labov, William. 2001. *Principles of Linguistic Change*, vol. 2, *Social Factors.* Oxford: Basil Blackwell.

Labov, William. 2013. *The Language of Life and Death.* Cambridge: Cambridge University Press.

Labov, William. 2018. The role of the *Avant garde* in linguistic diffusion. *Language Variation and Change* 30: 1–21.

Labov, William. 2020. What has been built on Empirical Foundations. In Hans C. Boas and Marc Pierce (eds.), *New Directions for Historical Linguistics.* Leiden: Brill, 42–57.

Labov, William, Sharon Ash, and Charles Boberg. 2006. *Atlas of North American English: Phonology and Sound Change.* Berlin: Mouton de Gruyter.

Labov, William, Mark Karan, and Corey Miller. 1991. Near mergers and the suspension of phonemic contrast. *Language Variation and Change* 3: 33–74.

Labov, William, Ingrid Rosenfelder, and Josef Fruehwald. 2013. One hundred years of sound change in Philadelphia: Linear incrementation, reversal, and reanalysis. *Language* 89: 30–65.

Labov, William, Malcah Yaeger, and Richard Steiner. 1972. *A Quantitative Study of Sound Change in Progress.* Philadelphia: US Regional Survey.

Lerner, Murray (dir.) 1967. *Festival.* n.p.: Patchke Productions.

Lerner, Murray (dir.). 1968. *From Mao to Mozart.* n.p.: Hopewell Foundation.

Macaulay, Ronald K. S. 1991. *Locating Dialect in Discourse.* Oxford: Oxford University Press.

Macaulay, Ronald K. S. 2005. *Extremely Common Eloquence: Constructing Scottish Identity through Narrative.* Amsterdam: Rodopi.

Miller, Perry. 1958–59. The New England conscience. *American Scholar* 28: 49–58.

Milroy, Lesley. 1987. *Observing and Analysing Natural Language.* Oxford: Blackwell.

Montgomery, Michael. 1989. Exploring the roots of Appalachian English. *English World-Wide* 10: 227–78.

Montgomery, Michael. 2014. The historical background and nature of the Englishes in Appalachia. In Amy D. Clark and Nancy M. Hayward (eds.), *Talking Appalachian: Voice, Identity and Community.* Lexington: University Press of Kentucky, 25–53.

Naro, Anthony J. 1981. The social and structural dimensions of a syntactic change. *Language* 57: 63–98.

Newman, Michael. 2014. *New York City English*. Boston: DeGruyter Mouton.

Poplack, Shana. 1989. The care and handling of a mega-corpus. In Fasold, R. and D. Schiffrin (eds.), *Language Change and Variation*. Amsterdam: Benjamins. 411–451.

Ochs, Elinor, Merav Shohet, Belinda Campos, and Margaret Beck. 2011. Coming together at dinner: A study of working families. In Kathleen Christensen and Barbara Schneider (eds.), *Workplace Flexibility*. Ithaca, NY: Cornell University Press, 57–70.

Read, Allen Walker. 1963. The first stage in the history of O.K. *American Speech* 38: 5–27.

Reed, Paul. 2014. Inter- and intra-generational /aɪ/ monophthongization, indexicality, and Southern Appalachian identity. *Southern Journal of Linguistics* 38: 159–93.

Rosenfelder, Ingrid, Joseph Fruehwald, Keelan Evanini, and Jiahong Yuan. 2012. FAVE (Forced alignment and vowel extraction) program suite. http://fave.ling.upenn.edu.

Sankoff, David, and Gillian Sankoff. 1973. Sample survey methods and computer-assisted analysis in the study of grammatical variation. In Regna Darnell (ed.), *Canadian Languages in Their Social Context*. Edmonton: Linguistic Research, 7–64.

Sankoff, Gillian. 2018. Before there were corpora. In Suzanne Evans Wagner and Isabelle Buchstaller (eds.), *Panel Studies of Variation and Change*. New York: Routledge, 21–51.

Sankoff, Gillian, and Henrietta J. Cedergren. 1971. Les contraintes linguistiques et sociales de l'élision du l chez les Montréalais. In M. Boudreault and F. Moehren (eds.), *Proceedings of the XIII International Congress of Romance Linguistics and Philology*. Québec: Presses de l'Université Laval, 1101–16.

Scherre, Maria Marta Pereira, and Anthony J. Naro. 1981. Marking in discourse: "Birds of a feather." *Language Variation and Change* 3: 23–32.

Schilling, Natalie. 2013. *Sociolinguistic Fieldwork*. Cambridge: Cambridge University Press.

Shuy, Roger, Walt Wolfram, and William K. Riley. 1967. *A Study of Social Dialects in Detroit*. Final Report, Project 6–1347. Washington, DC: Office of Education.

Strassel, Stephanie, et al. 2003. SLX Corpus of Classic Sociolinguistic Interviews LDC2003T15. Web download. Philadelphia: Linguistic Data Consortium.

Tagliamonte, Sali. 2006. *Analysing Sociolinguistic Variation*. Cambridge: Cambridge University Press.

Trudgill, Peter. 1974. *The Social Differentiation of English in Norwich*. Cambridge: Cambridge University Press.

Voegelin, Carl, and Zellig Harris. 1951. A method for determining intelligibility among dialects of natural languages. *Proceedings of the American Philosophical Society* 95: 322–29.

Wainfur, Rob. 2012. *Jaws: Memories From Martha's Vineyard* book review. The Bearded Trio. October 10. www.thebeardedtrio.com/2012/10/jaws-memories-from-marthas-vineyard.html.

Weber, Max. 1948. *The Protestant Ethic and the Spirit of Capitalism*. Translated by Talcott Parsons. Charles Scribner's Sons.

Weinreich, Uriel, William Labov, and Marvin Herzog. 1968. Empirical foundations for a theory of language change. In Winfred Lehmann and Yakov Malkiel (eds.), *Directions for Historical Linguistics*. Austin: University of Texas Press, 97–195.

Wolfram, Walt. 2013. African American speech in Southern Appalachia. In Nancy Hayward and Amy Clark (eds.), *Talking Appalachian: Voice, Identity, and Community*. Lexington: University of Kentucky Press, 81–93.

Wolfram, Walt, and Donna Christian. 1976. *Appalachian Speech*. Arlington: Center for Applied Linguistics.

Acknowledgments

The present form of this Element is the joint work of myself and my wife and colleague Gillian Sankoff, whose collaboration was essential from the start. We reviewed many interviews together before finally deciding on the ten speakers you will hear, and she has taken the entire responsibility for editing and transcribing the sound files. She urged me to write the section "Growing Up in New Jersey," and to organize the sections as a journey through the series of research projects I undertook. If this work is an accounting of what I have done, it demands even more an accounting from someone who has planned the route and knows where it is going.

I am grateful to series editor Raj Mesthrie, not only for his encouragement, support, and good advice all along the way, but for his own research that has contributed to making sociolinguistics a truly international enterprise. Thanks also to associate editor Valerie Fridland for her close reading and helpful suggestions, and to an anonymous reader whose comments helped in clarifying a number of important points. Penny Eckert has emerged as the most resolute force in our understanding of the social dimension of language variation and change, and her influence appears on every page of this work.

For thoughtful comments on the manuscript, I thank Meredith Tamminga, Joe Fruchwald, Sali Tagliamonte, and Alice Goffman. Thanks also to Frank Scalpone, who helped me recognize the world that I emerged from, for his many decades of friendship. The late Chris Cieri saved me from the disorganization of time, facilitating my use of the digitized archival materials, and Jamison Labov helped with various issues in production. We are also grateful to our friends and colleagues Mark Liberman and Ronald Kim who alerted us to errors we had missed earlier. The interviewing skills of the late Ann Bower have preserved a coherent view of the South Philadelphia speech community in its many aspects. The interview with Gloria Stein was conducted with consummate skill by Chérie Francis and Paul Dietz. Julia Ford and her team at Cambridge University Press have been a pleasure to work with. Lastly, I am grateful to the very large number of people who opened their doors to the strangers from God knows where, and said what they had to say to produce such an eloquent result.

Cambridge Elements ⁼

Sociolinguistics

Rajend Mesthrie

University of Cape Town

Rajend Mesthrie is Emeritus Professor and past head of Linguistics and Research Chair at the University of Cape Town. He was President of the Linguistics Society of Southern Africa (2002–2009) and of the International Congress of Linguists (2013–2018). Among his publications are *The Cambridge Handbook of Sociolinguistics* and *World Englishes* (with R. Bhatt). He was a co-editor of *English Today* and editor of the Key Topics in Sociolinguistics series.

Valerie Fridland

University of Nevada, Reno

Valerie Fridland is a Professor at the University of Nevada, Reno. She is author of *Like, Literally, Dude: Arguing for the Good in Bad English*, co-author of *Sociophonetics*, and lead editor for the *Speech in the Western States* series. Her blog, Language in the Wild, appears with *Psychology Today*, and her lecture series, Language and Society, is available through The Great Courses.

About the Series

Sociolinguistics is a vital and rapidly growing subfield of linguistics that draws on linguistics, sociology, social psychology, anthropology and cultural studies. The topics covered in *Cambridge Elements in Sociolinguistics* will showcase how language is shaped by societal interactions and in turn how language is a central part of social processes.

Cambridge Elements ≡

Sociolinguistics

Elements in the Series

Printed in the United States
by Baker & Taylor Publisher Services